BASED ON THE THAMES TELEVISION CHILDREN'S SERIES WITH PRESENTERS . .

Susan Stranks.

Pete Brady

Tony Bastable

MAGPIE

ANNUAL-2

MAGPIE ANNUAL—2© 1970 Thames Television Ltd. Published in Great Britain by World Distributors (Manchester) Ltd., 12 Lever Street, Manchester M60 1TS. No material may be reproduced without the written consent of the Publisher. Text printed and bound by Purnell & Sons Ltd., Paulton (Somerset) and London. Cover printed by Oval Press Ltd., London S.E.5. SBN 7235 0096 7. Special Photography by Mike Cumper and J. Luthwaite.

THIS IS MAGPIE!

FIVE PEOPLE sit motionless at the long desk in the narrow control room. Their eyes shift from one to another of the nine flickering monitor screens that face them, and the bold sweep-hand of a wall clock counts off the dwindling seconds.

The atmosphere is tense. It could be the countdown to blastoff for the launch of a vital new spaceprobe. But it isn't. This scene happens twice a week, Tuesdays and Thursdays, in the final moments before another edition of MAGPIE goes live on transmission!

Where does it all begin? Basically, with the five researchers who spend most of their time looking for interesting items suitable for the programme. They follow up all sorts of promising stories, perhaps suggested by short snippets in magazines, local newspapers or even by viewers. They seek out people with curious hobbies, people with odd pets. People who do strange jobs and people who live in extraordinary places. They find out all there is to know about exciting events, rescue organisations, expeditions, adventures.

The researchers come to MAGPIE Producer Sue Turner with their ideas, and Sue gets to work planning programmes with the items she judges suitable. She works two weeks ahead, though every programme can and often does change right up to the last moment. One of her responsibilities is to make sure that each programme is balanced—that is, that the items for presentation are nice and varied.

Sue Turner produces a 'running order' for each programme. It's a sort of script—although a script as such can't be used in MAGPIE, for the simple reason that interviews with people can't be written out on paper beforehand. But the running order gives a breakdown of programme content, and includes an approximation of the time allowed for each separate item.

"This timing is absolutely vital," says Sue. "I suppose many viewers think that all television programmes go out from the same studio. They probably imagine that a show begins, runs to the half-way mark, then stops while someone presses a button and transmits commercials. Actually, it's not like that at all!

"Commercials are transmitted from a studio miles away from ours, and they *have* to go out at a fixed time. This means that our two segments of MAGPIE *must* end at an exact time—a time measured to a fraction of a second."

Measuring that time is all very well if you've got a pre-recorded programme on video-tape. Such a programme is made days before, and there's a chance to cut and edit so that the timing ends up perfect. But MAGPIE goes out live, and timing can be complicated by guests on the show who talk too much, animals that escape and waste precious moments running loose around the studio, and (happily, it seldom happens) unexpected trouble with camera or sound equipment.

Obviously, there has to be a certain amount of rehearsal and run-through to minimise the likelihood of anything awkward happening during a transmission. It's because of this that the work of putting MAGPIE on screen for thirty minutes actually takes a whole day in the studio.

It begins at eleven in the morning, with a camera rehearsal involving most of the team concerned, but it isn't usually until after lunch that Sue Turner goes down to Teddington from the London offices of Thames Television.

She arrives in time for the 'stagger'. "That," laughs Sue, "is when everyone staggers through a rough rehearsal of the actual programme."

It's two p.m. Perhaps fourteen hundred hours would be a better term, in view of the 'mission control' atmosphere at the studio.

Behind the desk, the five are in their seats. The Operational Supervisor, in charge of transmission technicalities. The Vision Mixer, selecting the pictures at the Director's command. The Director. The Production Assistant with her stopwatches. The Producer. To the left, in a separate room, the Sound Engineers. Beyond them, 'Racks'—their responsibility to make sure that the pictures reaching your screens are of top quality. On the right, the sound room.

The Director speaks into a microphone, through which instructions are relayed to the Floor Manager in the studio below. His job is to watch over everything down there under the Director's instructions. The four cameras, the huge boom microphone, the timing of each item. In one corner of his studio, a table is rigged to display the collection of police badges that's been

Make up—an all important preparation for the T.V. cameras.

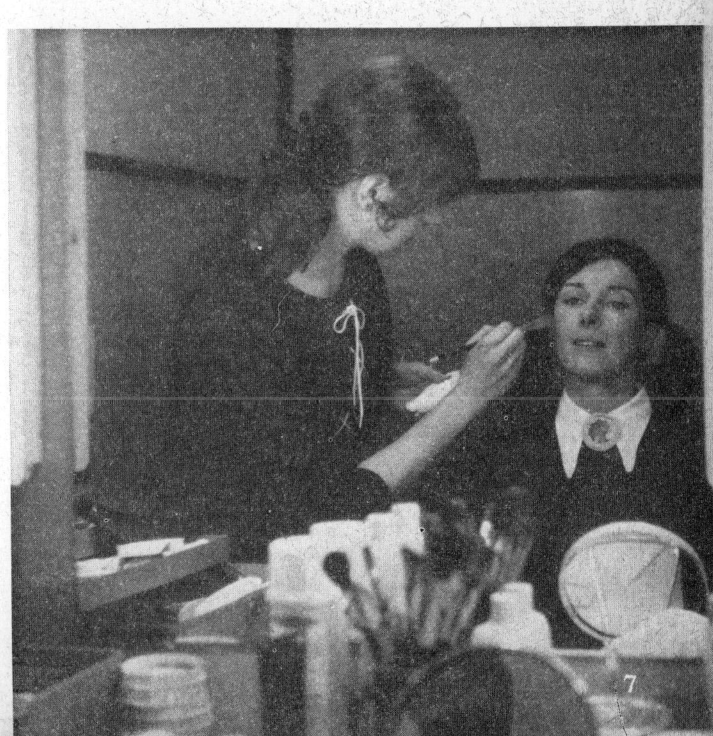

A view of the transmission control room—nerve centre of the programme.

made by an Inspector of the Kent County Constabulary. In another corner, the side table and chairs where Tony Bastable will interview England Football Captain Bobby Moore, and where three invited viewers will ask the star questions. On one side, an impressive 'set' built to look like the courtyard of a Tudor mansion where Susan Stranks will present costume of the period. Next time, the set-up will be different. Today it's like this. And the place seethes with camera, sound and lighting teams, people from wardrobe and make-up, presenters and the people they'll be interviewing.

In the control room, four of the black and white screens show different transmitted pictures from each camera. Two of them show similar shots in colour. The one at the top—the master screen—is to show the picture for transmission, and it's blank.

The Production Assistant begins a countdown. "Five, four, three, two, one . . . zero!"

"Go!" This from the Director.

Now the top screen is live, in full colour. The 'titles' (the drawing of Murgatroyd) flashes up, and the introductory music comes over the sound room. Over all, the voice of the Production Assistant, now on another countdown that comes to zero again as the title fades and the Director calls for camera one.

Instantly, Pete Brady's face is there, introducing the Police Inspector.

He's got three minutes, but after two, the Director calls for a halt, and disappears from the control room. Seconds later, the Director's down in the studio, visible on the monitors, explaining to Pete and the Inspector that their hands are obscuring the badges as they're brought into close-up on camera two.

Now we're off again, and the interview runs through. The running order specifies that the next item on the list is a ten second introduction by Tony Bastable leading into seven minutes of Telecine—that's jargon for film . . . a filmed item that shows Tony's visit to a riding school for disabled children.

"Cue to Telecine. One minute." This is the Production Assistant. One of the monitors flickers, ready to screen the film.

"They're over-running."

Pete and his Inspector have got too involved about the badges! The Production Assistant has cued them. "Two minutes left."

"One minute."

"Thirty seconds."

"Over. Ten seconds . . . fifteen . . . " The instructions reach the Floor Manager, and Pete knows he's beyond the limit by hand-signals.

"Let him go on," says the Producer. One of the monitors is ready with a shot of Tony, waiting for the signal to begin.

Pete closes the interview with the police officer . . . "Camera four" raps the Director. Now Tony's in action, against the eternal countdown from the control room. He leads into the film, and there's a moment of relaxation. Pre-recorded, everyone knows exactly how long that's going to run.

There's a swift work-out to suggest cuts in Pete's interview so that it comes down to schedule.

Ever-watchful, the Production Assistant cues the end of the film, and as it ends, Tony comes back on camera to wind up the first half of the programme.

"Stand by with scanner." The Director orders the titles to be monitored . . . 'Magpie — Gone to Roost'. "Stand by grams." This is for the music.

"Titles running . . . "

"Five, four, three, two, one . . . zero."

Relax again. "Two minutes thirty-five seconds commercial break."

On the monitors, cameras can be seen getting into position for the second half of the show. A babble comes up from the intercom . . .

"Quiet in the studio, please! One minute to go!"

"Thirty seconds . . . "

Zero. And back comes Pete to introduce Susan in Elizabethan costume. She runs through, describing her dress—even though she's not in costume yet. There's another over-run, and another problem besides. The scene is dramatised, in that Susan is acting the part of a lady of the period, expecting guests.

"Cue bell!" This is the Director, looking annoyed. "Where's that bell?" Looks round towards the sound room.

Belatedly, the sound of a bell is fed into the sound system, and Susan, waiting for it, bursts out laughing. "Er . . . yes! I've got guests . . . *at last*!"

Notes are made. *That* mustn't happen when the programme goes out!

"Cue VTR." This is as Tony comes on after Susan to introduce Bobby Moore. The VTR is a Videotape recording that shows Bobby scoring a spectacular goal.

The VTR begins to run on one of the monitors, and comes up on the transmission screen, dead on cue.

"And *through*!"

Camera four comes back with Tony as the film ends, and the interview begins. It runs to time, and the three guest viewers run through their questions without any nervousness at all . . . a tribute to the atmosphere of calm on the studio floor . . . something of a contrast to the busy, hectic air of the control room!

Now Pete and Susan come back in, and the wind-up of the show begins. The final countdown starts, and as titles and music are cued again, the lights come up in the control room.

It's three-fifteen, and now everyone departs to the canteen as the cameras go into 'line-up', which is a necessary technical period for them to work at maximum efficiency.

Problems are thrashed out. Adjustments made. Director and Producer read off the

An outdoor sequence being prepared for Magpie.

mass of notes they've scribbled on their typewritten running orders.

Then it's back for the whole thing over again . . . after a session in make-up and a struggle into the right clothes.

This is dress rehearsal, then, and at four-fifteen on the dot, the cameras go into action.

This time, there are no over-runs. There are minor problems . . . a little more super-imposed bird-song to back up Susan's item. A touch of anti-glare spray on the chromium fronts of the interview chairs so that they don't dazzle the cameras. Minor points on sound and camera.

At a quarter to five, the whole team breaks for tea, and the real wind-up begins for the live transmission. The feeling isn't exactly tense. It mustn't be, or the people being interviewed would become nervous. Every-one, even Producer and Director, who have a *right* to be extra nervous, seems at ease, and there's relaxation by the time the call comes for the return to the studio.

But this is the real thing! Isolated in the control room, the five at the desk sit there tensely. In front of them, researchers who've done the background digging for the items on the show are equally keyed-up. All eyes are on those screens.

"Five minutes before transmission." To the right of the Production Assistant, on the facing wall, a rev-counter begins to wind away minutes and seconds.

"Three and a half minutes." The screens come on.

"One minute."

The Director leans forward. "Good luck, studios."

"Good luck, *everybody*!" That's Sue Turner, and she holds up her hands, every finger crossed!

We're on! The Director is speaking quietly, her cues going down to the Floor Manager. Titles flash up, and the music begins. The watchers in the control room seem to hold their breath, as though any word or movement would wreck the whole thing . . .

But there's Pete on the monitor now, cool as the proverbial cucumber. The Inspector, looking as though he appears on television every day of his life.

Then . . . "He's going to over-run!" A trace of urgency from the Production Assistant. One imagines the Floor Manager holding up five fingers in front of Pete . . . but there's no hint of worry on the screen.

"Over-run! Five seconds. Ten. Fifteen . . . "

Pete ends, and expertly, Tony takes up the lost time. The Telecine comes on . . . runs . . . fades out. And then the crippling final seconds before the rigidly fixed moment when the first half *must* end!

"Five . . . four . . . three . . . " Will he make it? *Will he*?

"Two . . . one . . . Zero!" He's there! Dead on time, the screens fade for the commercial break!

The second half begins. Nothing—absolutely nothing goes wrong. It's perfect all the way. But *still* there's that dreadful feeling as the clock—master of everything—knocks away those precious seconds. It seems impossible, as the time charges towards the end, that the programme could finish on time! But it does, and bodies seem to go limp in the control room.

"Well done, everyone. Thank you!" The Director gets up, and there's laughing and joking. "Did you see?" "Well, *I* thought..." "Wasn't Bobby Moore *marvellous* . . . "

The tension is over . . . for a while. And at home, millions of viewers think over what they've seen. They've enjoyed the programme, thanks to the faceless team who, behind the presenters, work so hard to make it all possible! ■

Producer	**Sue Turner**
Directors	**David Hodgson** **Diana Potter** **Robert Reed**
Designer	**Philip Blowers**
Film Editors	**Bob Harvey** **Rosemary MacLoughlin**
Researchers	**Valerie Brayden** **Jackie Colkett** **David McFarlane** **Martin Robertson** **Mick Robertson**

ON SAFARI

—THE STATELY WAY

One of the unhappiest things about the growth of civilisation is that, as mankind finds he needs more and more room to live, he begins to take over the wide open spaces, and uses them to build houses and factories. Of course, it's all very necessary, but it's not very nice for all the wild animals who find themselves driven from their homes. This sort of thing even happens in Africa, where the once enormous stretches of open bushland are gradually becoming smaller and smaller. The answer doesn't lie in zoos, with their cramped, depressing cages. It lies in the construction of natural parks and reserves, places like the one described here.

HENRY FREDERICK THYNNE, 6th Marquess of Bath, lives in a palatial stately home called Longleat, some five miles out of Warminster and close to the Somerset border. He was the first peer of the realm to open his doors to the public—a step he took in 1949.

The reason for what was then a revolutionary move was one of simple economics. Without public support, he simply could not have afforded to keep a house and estate such as Longleat in good repair.

It was a meeting with Jimmy Chipperfield, a man whose family history had been for over 300 years tied up with animals, that first gave birth to the idea of opening a lion reserve at Longleat, for Jimmy Chipperfield, with a lifetime of experience of African big-game, knew that the establishment of a reserve in Britain would be a practical proposition. More than that, it would be a wonderful example of progress in the fight to conserve wild animals.

There were difficulties and setbacks, but in the spring of 1966, the Lions of Longleat became fact, and the 100-acre area, enclosed by two miles of twelve-foot high safety fence with a two-foot overhang, was opened to the public, who experienced for the first time two miles of Safari driving along a road frequently criss-crossed by their padding majesties, the Kings of The Jungle!

Longleat quickly won the admiration of leading zoologists. Local and national authorities, eager to co-operate, made possible the development of Longleat as a natural home for many more species of wild animals, and now there is a further 100-acre enclosure where giraffe, zebra, antelope and ostrich roam free. Again, hundreds of African baboons in massive family colonies live in another 10-acre enclosure, and there are hippos and sea-lions in a lake that surrounds the island stronghold of the chimpanzees.

The eighteenth-century landscaping expert, Lancelot 'Capability' Brown, who laid out Longleat's delightful park, would undoubtedly have approved of the wild-life reserve, because of the enjoyment it gives.

A family can take a drive through the lion enclosure, seeing the noble animals at close quarters in perfect safety. The only condition is that car windows mustn't be fully opened, for although the lions look placid enough, they're wild, and are never to be trusted! Cars mustn't stop, either . . . though if they break down, there's a foolproof procedure—the continual sounding of the horn—that brings help from a patrol vehicle with its attendant hunters, men trained in dealing with big game.

The Longleat lions are perfectly at home in the English climate. In fact, they are rather more active in the winter months than they are in the summer. They grow thicker coats to protect them from the weather, and they have draught-proof shelters to keep warm in when the cold winds are blowing too hard. They eat about one and a half tons of meat every week, and it's all supplied on the bone, so that they have the chance to exercise their teeth, and aren't tempted to upset their stomachs by swallowing whole chunks at once. The young ones are especially well off, as they get extra vitamins to make them grow strong.

The other main enclosure—the East African Game Park—rivals the lion reserve in popularity, and the reason is very obvious. Here, the visitor can wander about freely—even picnic—and observe the animals at the closest of possible quarters.

They mustn't be touched or fed, for they are all fairly easily frightened, and things like buns and chocolate bars don't do their digestive systems any good, but they'll come close, all of them . . . from the impressive, seventeen-foot tall Rothschild's Giraffe to the zebras—the Common Zebra and Hartmann's Mountain Zebra. The latter species is practically extinct in the wild state, which all goes to prove how beneficial places like Longleat are.

There are various species of antelope, some Ankole cattle, ostriches, pelicans, East African crowned cranes and marabou storks, and all of them grow more and more eager to pose for the thousands of pictures that are taken every year by tourists!

Anyone who drives through Monkey Jungle—the enclosure where the baboons live—has to be very careful not to open the car doors or attempt to feed the baboons. The animals are delightfully inquisitive, and love to come and perch on the bonnet, staring in through the windscreen . . . but they're rather unpredictable, and have a disconcerting habit of biting!

It's the same with the chimpanzees. They may look lovable and mischievous when they're young, but as they reach the age of seven or eight, they begin to exhibit nasty tempers. That's why, at Longleat, they live on an island, where they're fed with fruit, vegetables and bread, and find themselves berries growing on the bushes there. Some of them throw things at passing boats, and erupt into comical but very real rage when their missiles fail to reach the target!

Sea-lions follow the boats on the lake, keeping up a continuous display of swimming and diving, and there are a couple of docile hippos, Arnold and Freda, around two and a half tons each, ready to yawn for fruit that the park wardens throw to them. Apart from these titbits, they enjoy enormous quantities of hay, grass, root vegetables and bread as well.

Last but not least, there's a Pets Corner, where all sorts of creatures from parrots to rabbits, from guinea-pigs to lion cubs, entertain the youngest visitors.

But apart from sheer entertainment, Longleat actively supports the East African Wildlife Society's efforts to preserve game in Africa. The reserve has been a worthwhile example to other similar schemes that have been started both in Britain and abroad, and if the animals could speak, they'd be certain to agree! ■

THE COSTUMES OF THE COUNTRY

HANDS UP anyone who doesn't like togging up in fancy dress!

What, no hands? That isn't surprising, because nearly everyone loves dressing up, especially in old-fashioned costumes! After all, it only takes a change of clothes, and you become prince or pirate, Queen Elizabeth or the Queen of Sheba, Robin Hood, roundhead, Regency belle or Regency beau.

The odd thing is, that all the dramatic, glamorous costumes you'd love to wear were once the everyday clothes of the period to which they belonged. It's quite likely that in a couple of hundred years time, people will be going to fancy-dress balls in bowler hats and pin-stripe suits, or in mini-skirts or maxi coats. *And* they'll say "wouldn't it have been wonderful to have lived in the 1970s and worn these things all the time"!

If we go right back to the days of the Saxons, we find that costume was very simple. Men and women wore clothes that were basically the same—a loose tunic with a slit down the front, an undertunic like a long vest, and long, baggy socks held up by criss-crossed tapes. The only differences between the sexes' clothes were that the women's undertunics usually came down to their feet, while the men's ended at their knees. And the men generally wore a belt—which served both to keep their

Left: Pete's always at home on horseback, even when he's all done up in the uniform of a cavalry officer of the 1640s! As for Tony, his Isaac Newton outfit of the 1700s is enough to make all the apples fall!

Right: Susan's costumes show off the elegance of 1430 (on the left) and the ornate Elizabethan style of 1585. How about those classic 'winkle-pickers' worn by mediaeval ladies!

tunics closed and as a handy anchorage for a dagger and a pouch. For formal wear, men and women would put on a cloak, fastened with a brooch on one shoulder. The man's ended clear of the ground, whereas the woman's was likely to trail behind in a two-foot train.

When the Normans came to Britain, the fashions remained almost the same. Perhaps the clothes were more elaborately embroidered, and head-coverings . . . hats and veils . . . were different.

In the early middle ages, there was a sort of up-and-down movement like the fashion in women's hemlines today. Only it applied to men and their 'braies'—the term then applied to breeches. These garments had in fact been favoured by many Saxons, and were loose trousers held up at the waist by a draw-string. Now, in the twelfth century, they began to rise above the knee, and the hose or stockings that covered them began to get longer and longer, until they reached the thigh. The men kept them in place with laces at the tops, which were threaded into the legs of the braies. The big fashion of the time was for richly decorated girdles in leather, looped around the waist of a surcote or tabard. These garments were plain and sleeveless, and they really needed the girdle to stop them looking like sacks!

It wasn't until the fourteenth century that the term fashion as we know it became interwound with costume. Tailoring had become much more advanced, and rich, embroidered materials were being more and more used. Around the 1330s, the fad came in for fitted clothes. Men took to wearing hip-length tunics, heavy with heraldic designs, and hose that were an absolute riot of colour! Sometimes, one leg would be quartered in red and blue, while the other was striped in green and yellow! The women were a little more sensible, and stuck to long, elegant, button-fronted gowns called 'cotehardies', where the decorations were usually confined to extravagant motifs on the 'tippets'—long, trailing pieces on the elbow-length sleeves. Naturally, as with any innovation of fashion, there were older people who did not like to wear these 'new fangled' clothes that showed the lines of their bodies. For them, there was the 'houppelande'—a voluminous sort of gown with a high neck, long, loose sleeves, and a hem that reached the ground.

In those days, there were two especial features of fashion—the one rather beautiful, the other absurd. Even though men were far greater peacocks than their ladies, it was the latter who wore magnificent head-dresses, hung with jewels and gold chain.

And the men? They went to ridiculous

lengths—literally—with the tips of their toes. The feet of their long hose were often extended into trailing points that must have threatened to trip them at every step. Sometimes these points were so unmanageably long that they had to be caught up and secured to a garter worn below the knee!

Now we come to padding, puffs and slashes—three terms which ought to conjure up visions of Henry VIII and the Tudor period.

If men were peacocks before, they were birds of paradise now, and those who could afford it were weighed down by rich velvets worn over a formidable structure of chest and shoulder padding that must have been designed to ape the King's squat, square figure.

The tunic was now termed a 'doublet', and had a square neck to show off the shirt underneath. The sleeves were puffed out with padding and slashed—that is cut and edged with jewels so that folds of the shirtsleeves could be pulled out and displayed. The doublet ended at the waist, and was laced down to the long hose—which must have looked just like modern-day tights. Then there came the doublet-skirt, which was tied around the middle, and on top of all that, an overtunic or 'jerkin', which was again made of rich, heavy material, but was sleeveless. Very often, a man of fashion would wear a gown on top of all that—a long garment rather like a cloak.

Women of the time had their own problems, for it was during the Tudor period that corsets were first introduced. They were perfectly comfortable for those with good figures, but they must have been agony for the fashion-conscious to whom dieting was unknown! The shape of a lady's gown at the time was like a cone—and the material of it was kept that way by an undergarment known as a farthingale, hooped with whalebone. When you look at paintings made in this part of the sixteenth century, you'll often notice ornate, filigree containers hung on long chains from the belts around women waists. These are pomanders, which contained perfume. The town streets in those days smelled abominably, and so pomanders were essential to anyone with a sensitive nose!

The costume worn by a 'Regency Belle' about 1803. Although Britain was at war with France, the fashions of Napoleon's court were quick to catch on here. Note the high 'waist' of the empire line.

The Tudor style of costume kept its popularity, with various changes . . . lace ruffs, for example, longer, slashed breeches for the men, different hats and hairstyles . . . until the coming of The Stuarts. Or rather, until the coming of Charles I.

Everyone knows what a cavalier looks like—the falling lace at the neck, the gay, plumed hats, sleeves and knees dripping with more lace. His lady, though favouring lace as well, gained a certain amount of freedom as corset and farthingale passed out of fashion, and her long, rich skirt was often caught up in folds above the hem to show the layered underskirts.

After centuries of increasing finery, the halt had to come. It took Oliver Cromwell and his puritans to bring in stark, severe costume which, although based in cut on the styles of the times, were made of plain, unadorned black cloth, without a lace or a ribbon in sight. Mind you, it was only the extreme religous puritans who wore that kind of thing. There were many supporters of the Parliament cause who continued to copy the Royalist fashions.

A gentleman's coat of the period 1720-1740, made in french brocade silk. This style came to England from Germany.

An English dress, about 1760. The skirt was kept full by steel hoops sewn into an underskirt (far right).

Charles II and the restoration period brought back a positively ridiculous crop of fashions—many of them copied from France, where the King had been in exile. Ribbons and bows almost covered the men of the period, and it wasn't until the 1670s that things began to settle down a bit. One important introduction of the time was the periwig—a fashion that continued for more than a century, and must have been a boon to bald-headed men who found their shiny pates took the gilt off the effect of their magnificent clothes!

Wigs and hairpieces were worn by women as well as men, of course. The custom persisted into the eighteenth century, when hair sometimes became grotesque enough to be ridiculed in the press. Young men called 'macaronis' might wear wigs anything up to three feet in height—gravely running the risk of having them knocked askew by small boys armed with stones!

The eighteen century brought with it a style of dress, both for men and women, that would be hard to equal in terms of sheer dazzling, gorgeous display. Skirted coats in magnificent brocades, deeply cuffed, beautifully embroidered. Spectacular crinolines resplendent in taffeta, silk, satin and damask . . . This was the very peak of British fashion, never again to be attained.

The mid-eighteenth century saw the advent of the Empire line . . . Grecian-style dresses for the women, high waisted and bare-shouldered, and innocent of hoops under the skirt. For men, tight-fitting coats with tails, knee breeches and silk stockings that soon gave way to trousers cut full length. Colours were still bright, but embroidery was out. It was an age where flamboyance had given way to plain elegance.

Basically, men's clothing has changed very little from that day to this. Cut, styling, material and colour may have varied—but the basic principle of jacket, waistcoat and trousers is the same. As for women—well, fashion being what it is, changes of one kind and another happen every year. Bustles have been in and out. Hems have gone up, down, and up again. They even wear trousers! As a Saxon might say, the whole thing has turned full circle, and you can't tell one from the other until they open their mouths!

Never mind. It's easy enough to get away from the everyday clothes we wear. Some of us can go and hire things from a theatrical costumier; some of us can borrow old clothes from the attic trunk. Others can make pretty marvellous-looking outfits themselves out of odds and ends and the old curtains. *All* of us can dress up! ■

The best things in life are free!

How many collectors do you know? Dozens, probably, for nearly everyone collects something or other. It might be stamps, it might be silver. Maybe coins, maybe china. Furniture or figurines, paintings or pop records. Books or badges. But you know what they all say, these collectors? That collecting is one of the most rewarding hobbies a person can have!

THEY'RE RIGHT, OF COURSE. Each of them is able to look at his collection and derive real interest from it. His stamps will teach him, in the most pleasant way, bits and pieces of world history, of geography, of language. Any stamp collector worth his salt is always a mine of varied information. He'll know that the capital of Sierra Leone is Freetown, and he'll know where it is. What's more, he'll know what it looks like, what its inhabitants are like, and what they do for a living. And—like all his silver, china, coin and furniture collecting friends—he'll have had to pay for his knowledge.

But the fact is, you *can* make a collection—just as interesting and informative as any of those listed above—that will cost you practically nothing. What's more, the search for specimens will provide a stack of happy memories that will always be recalled every time you choose to look over what you've got.

There are dozens of things you can set out to collect on the cheap. There are leaves that can be had for the picking, to be mounted in exercise books and 'written up' with all the details you can find out about the parent tree. There are sea-shells to pack in cotton wool and identify against the beautiful drawings you can find in dozens of library books on the subject. There are train-numbers and car registrations . . . not much in themselves, but there's plenty of interest if you find yourself inspired to make a proper study of railways or cars in general. There are stones, pebbles and flints—all the things you can pick up literally anywhere!

There are an endless variety of matchbox labels.

Yes, they're *very* interesting, because . . . but well, there's so much about them that we've a special feature on pages 36 and 37!

Then, of course, there are labels. Without a shadow of doubt, matchbox labels run stamps a close second by way of interest and information, and collectors of them (known as phillumenists) are far more numerous than you might suppose. There are several societies for matchbox-label collectors in Britain—the largest being the British Matchbox Label and Booklet Society (Honorary Secretary, Mr J. H. Luker, 283/285 Worplesdon Road, Guildford, Surrey). This society caters for collectors all over the world and, naturally, matchbox labels can be either swapped or purchased through the organisation. However, matches are such an everyday commodity that it's perfectly possible to build up an enormous collection without spending a single copper. Your own friends, your relations, and their friends will usually save anything they come across, while you sit happily waiting for the specimens to come rolling in. Your equipment can be as ambitious as a loose-leaf stamp album, or it can be as simple as an exercise book. All you actually have to do, physically, is soak the labels off the boxes when you get them, and mount them—preferably with stamp hinges. You'll find boxes with 'wrap round' labels on . . . which must be kept intact, of course. The backs often have puzzles and tricks, horoscopes, recipes, facts and figures printed on them. Then you'll pick up foreign examples whenever anyone comes back from an overseas holiday. If the collecting bug really bites you, you'll find yourself drawn by some thrown-away box lying on the pavement . . . but here you have to be careful. Of course, some people aren't particularly fussy, but there's that old caution about 'you never know where it's been'! If you *must* pick up boxes in the street, add a touch of disinfectant to the warm water when you're soaking off the label.

Just as a side thought, anyone who finds specimens in the street is in good company.

Collecting cheese labels can be interesting. This one is more than appropriate.

One of the Kings of Siam—an avid phillumenist—startled his escorts on one of his visits to Britain by dashing across the road to pick up a particularly tempting and sought-after item! Actually, he nearly came to grief under the wheels of a London bus, but that's another story!

Matchbox labels are tremendously varied in type. When you begin swapping with other collectors, you'll come across labels used as propaganda . . . carrying slogans that encourage you to do all sorts of things from voting Communist to eating more fruit. Labels that rant and rave against the evils of alcohol, that teach road safety, that urge you to avoid forest fires or save waste paper. There's one—a Japanese example—that even sets out the pleasures of collecting matchbox labels!

There are labels portraying royalty (often incredibly badly, so that Kings and Queens end up looking like grotesque clowns). There are labels portraying buildings, costumes, works of art. Labels advertising airlines, beers, holiday resorts and clubs.

There are labels still in existence which have a historic story of their own . . . the labels from the days when the match industry was in its infancy. The wonderful thing about matchbox label collecting is that these early items, dating perhaps from the middle nineteenth century, are sometimes offered for sale through collectors' clubs . . . and bearing in mind their great age, they're extremely cheap! Real rarities may fetch seven or eight pounds (modest, remembering that postage stamp rarities often cost many thousands of pounds) but it's a happy thought that large sample packets of overseas matchbox labels are to be found in any hobby shop for a modest shilling or so.

Other label hobbies are legion. Cheese labels are nearly as popular as those from matchboxes, and can be bought in certain shops in packets. They're colourful, easy to find, and are usually helpful to anyone studying European languages, especially French. There is one cheese label—in fact it's Dutch—called 'Magpie', which makes the hobby worthwhile including in our list!

Then there are bottle labels, which don't supply very much in the way of interesting information, but are very colourful to collect.

You'll find orange-wrappers, melon and banana stickers, even sweet papers. They're all worth collecting if you feel like it. Some people even make collections of 'free offer' coupons cut from cereal cartons, tea-packets and so on.

There are beer mats, too—and a society for the collection of them. It's called The British Beer Mat Collectors' Society, and it's run by Derek Preedy from 142 Leicester Street, Wolverhampton in Staffordshire. It has a large junior section, and has branches all over the country that meet regularly to exchange mats and hold auctions. Collecting mats, for anyone under 18, is obviously a hobby that relies on the goodwill of parents and relatives, and if you think beer-mats aren't really respectable, be assured by the number of clergymen devoted to the hobby! The only trouble with beer-mats is space. A collection grows with alarming rapidity, and can quickly fill up odd drawers and carrier bags. There's one sad story about a chap in Folkestone who gathered together a wonderful collection

Drip mats come in all shapes and sizes.

in an old desk . . . only to have it attacked by woodworm! Tragically, the little creatures seemed to prefer the flavour of his mats to the flavour of the desk, and he suffered the ruin of his whole collection!

One type of cheap collection that can grow extremely absorbing is the collection of postmarks. It has its own worldwide company of devotees, and there's a very interesting book on the subject called simply 'Postmark Collecting', by R. K. Forster. It seems to be in every public library, and is well worth reading.

It's no use relying on your daily visit by the postman to build up a collection. To be sure of anything really interesting turning up, you *must* beg help from perhaps a relative or friend of the family who is used to dealing with heaps of mail. Anyone in business is a good bet. Bankers, publishers, people who work in mail-order houses are of course the best. Once you've persuaded them to keep envelopes for you, you're under way.

What's so interesting about postmarks? Several things. You occasionally come across commemorative marks—special frankings on envelopes posted from exhibitions, for example. But there are also postmarks that include 'slogans'—printed panels to the left of the stamp itself that advertise all sorts of things from the beauties of a seaside resort to the need for clear addressing. Thames T.V. once actually used Magpie on its frank.

Then there are the place names themselves. What a fantastic selection of curiously named places there are in the world! Take Battlefield, for example . . . or Box's Shop. Or British Legion Village, Clock Face, Decoy, Good Easter, Forty Foot or Foxholes. And *they're* all in Britain, so they shouldn't be hard to come by!

Find some person who is used to getting overseas mail, and you've got the means of starting a *fantastic* collection of unusual names! You may find Difficult, Devil's Slide, Dime Box, Love, Money, Midnight Tree, Peculiar, Fireworks, Bangs, Sleepy Eye or Bill's Place from America. You might happen across The Lagoon, The Sisters, or Come By Chance from Australia. Piggs Peak or Cookhouse from South Africa. Go Home or Ta-Ta Creek from Canada. The varieties are endless!

Some collectors try to arrange their collections in humorous sequences . . . pairing up place-names like Good (USA) and Bad (India), Ham (France) and Sandwich (England). Or they can sometimes set whole strings of postmarks side by side, to make up a sentence. . . .

For example, as the result of a competition held by an American magazine in 1949, someone managed to find twelve postmarks that read 'Friday Likely Tobe Chilly Little Sunshine Mininum Tempe Rat Ural Bee Forty Four.'

So much for our selection of cheap collections. There must be many, many more . . . but whatever you decide to go for, you can be sure of one thing. Every time you find an item that's exactly what you've been after for a long time, the pleasure you'll feel will be *just* as great as the joy of any millionaire philatelist, art-addict or furniture-fiend!

MURGATROYD'S MIND-BOGGLERS!

What's a mind-boggler? Why, something that makes the mind boggle, of course! Like these pictures. Fearsome-looking things, aren't they? Well, are they monsters from outer space? Or are they ordinary, everyday objects photographed terribly close-up from odd angles? Make your guesses, letting your mind boggle just as much as it likes, and finally turn to page 75 for the correct answers!

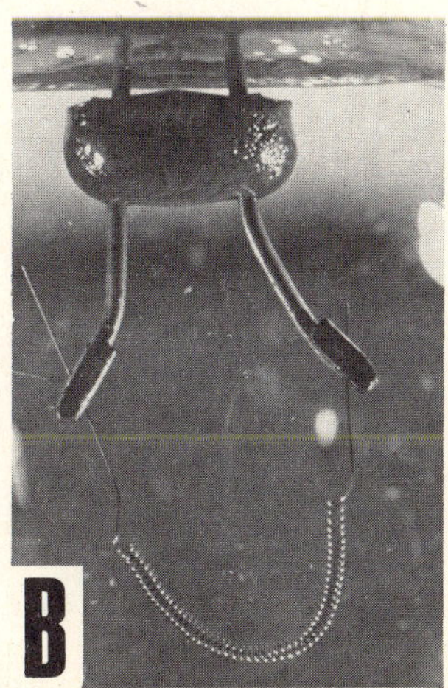

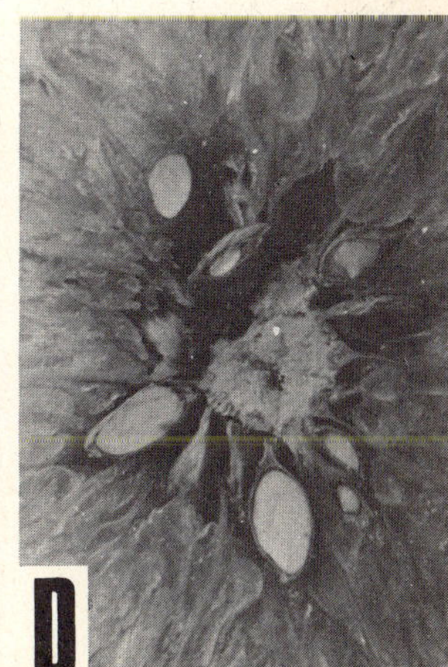

IT DOESN'T MATTER TUPPENCE if your name isn't Alexander . . . you can still have a Ragtime Band! There's no guarantee that delighted impresarios will come flocking with recording contracts, and you're hardly likely to gain fame and fortune and appear at the top of the hit parade . . . but you *can* make music that's fun and what's more, play it on instruments that you can knock up yourself out of odds and ends!

First, enlist the aid of half-a-dozen or so friends, and set aside about half an hour for the preparation of your instruments. It's best, first of all, to decide who is going to play what, and split the group up into two parts. Three of you will play the 'lead', or melody instruments, and the rest will handle the 'background', or rhythm section. For the lead musicians, you must select people who have a good ear for music. In other words, if they can sing in tune, then they're likely to be ideal.

The simplest and strongest lead instrument is naturally the good old comb and paper . . . simply a comb folded inside one layer of thin paper, preferably wrapping tissue. Whoever plays it simply has to hold it to his lips and hum through it, producing a trumpeting sort of buzz.

Then there's the 'pin piano'. You take a strip of wood six inches long, and drive eight long pins into it. You push the first in a little way, the second a little more, the third even more than that, and so on.

When you've finished, you'll find that the long pins, when plucked with a fork, give low notes, while the short ones give high notes. It shouldn't be difficult to adjust the pins so that they make a perfect doh-ray-me scale when plucked in sequence. Don't worry if you think they won't make enough noise to be heard . . . just rest the pin-piano on top of a stout tumbler, as you can see in the drawing, and you'll find the volume increases!

The third lead instrument is a bottle xylophone, and for this you'll need eight old mineral water bottles, some string, and any kind of wooden frame. Try borrowing the family clothes horse, for example. Again, you can see from the drawing how the instrument should look. You'll notice that there is some water in each of the bottles, each one being filled to a different level. The idea is that each bottle produces a different note when struck with a wooden spoon (lightly, mind! No spirited hammering, or you'll end up in a mess!) As with the pin-piano, you have to experiment with the water levels to obtain a true musical scale, and it should be possible to arrange things so that the bottles produce the same notes as the pins.

There you are, then. The lead instruments are ready, and now it's the turn of the rhythm section.

The scope is very wide here (so there can be as many rhythm players as you have room for). The most important member must be the drummer, and there's no sense in having a crash-bang-wallop merchant slogging his heart away with spoons on a pan. Far too noisy for the rest of the band! Take a suitcase and tie down a length of brown paper, or even newspaper, over it. Then arm your drummer with a pair of clothes brushes, and get him to move them rhythmically across the paper. It sounds very effective—and as a matter of interest, there were some real-life records made in 1929 by a group called The Mound City Blue Blowers that actually featured this very instrument!

You've probably heard maracas featured with Latin-American bands . . . dry gourds

filled with beans. You can easily make your own by popping a handful of rice-grains inside an empty plastic bottle and stoppering it.

If you're really ambitious, try making a tea-chest bass. Getting hold of a tea-chest from the grocer is probably the most difficult part, but if he's nice and friendly you'll be able to go ahead and fix up an arrangement with stout cord and a broomhandle, just as shown in the drawing. Plucking the cord produces a variety of notes according to your pull on the handle. A few minutes of experiment will show how it's done.

Anyone still without an instrument? Make up a variety of bamboo scraper-sticks . . . lengths of garden cane with notches cut close together. They're played by running a pencil along them.

That's it! Dish out more combs-and-papers to anyone else who feels competent to play, and start making music. Pick tunes that everyone knows, and you'll find that your ragtime band swings happily ever after! Incidentally, don't be discouraged if the dog begins to howl. Console yourself with the idea that he's only trying to join in!

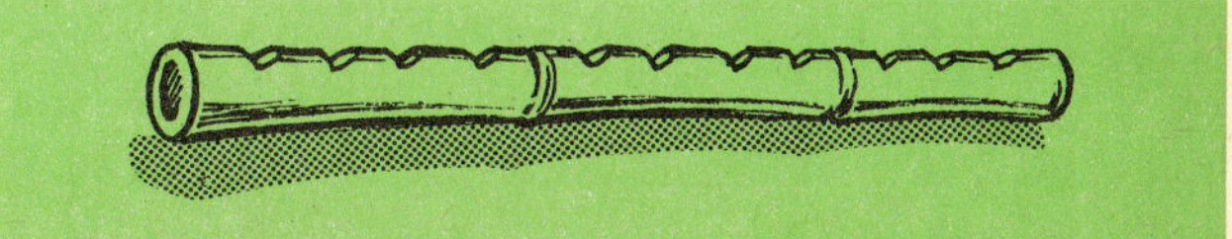

Smoke is just one of the many difficulties firemen encounter.

SUDDENLY, YOU'RE WIDE awake. For a moment, you're not sure why . . . and then you're aware of the strange, pinkish glow on the bedroom ceiling! The curtains are open . . . the street is dark and deserted . . . but there, behind the windows of the buildings opposite, you see it! *Fire!*

You don't waste a moment. Instantly, the whole house is roused, and someone's dialling 999. . . .

"Emergency. Which service do you require?"

"Fire!"

Immediately, the call is connected by direct line to the Fire Brigade Control Room covering your area. They ask the address. They ask for any details you can give them. And at the same time, they're pinpointing the exact location of the blaze. Now a message flashes to the nearest fire stations, and within seconds of the alert, the Brigade is on its way!

One of the world's largest fire-fighting organisations is the London Fire Brigade—an immense team that stands ready at all times to deal with emergencies from Barnet to Biggin Hill, from Hayes to Hornchurch. One hundred and thirteen fire stations. Over six thousand men and women. More than five hundred vehicles. A hundred and ten miles of hose!

The London Fire Brigade is split up into three separate commands; northern, eastern and southern. The three commands are themselves split up into divisions, each with its separate headquarters. But the whole network comes under the supreme control of Brigade H.Q. at Lambeth.

The service was first properly organised in 1833, when a group of large insurance companies, each of which had maintained its own fire-fighting team up to that time, got together to set up the London Fire Engine Establishment, under the leadership of James Braidwood.

Many of the principles of firemanship devised by Braidwood still hold good today, but the rapid growth of London in those days was too much for him, and it soon became clear that a privately run organisation could not possibly cope. When Braidwood met his tragic death at a disastrous fire in Tooley Street in 1861, the Government stepped in, and in 1865, an Act of Parliament placed all the men, stations and equipment of the London Fire Engine Establishment under the control of the Metropolitan Board of Works. Early in 1866, the Metropolitan Fire Brigade was born!

The new man in charge, Captain (later Sir) Eyre Massey Shaw, was luckily a man of vision. Shaw introduced steam fire engines, and set up telegraph systems. More than that, he extended the network of street fire escape stations which he took over from the Royal Society for the Protection of Life from Fire. *And* he took on the responsibility of inspecting public buildings for fire risks . . . a part of the Brigade's work that is taken for granted today.

In those days, a fireman was paid 22/- per week—actually not a bad wage for the times. But he was on more or less continuous duty, and had to live at the fire station. He was respected and admired by the public, and on occasions even found himself rubbing elbows with royalty. The Prince of Wales, later to become King Edward VII, took a keen personal interest in the Fire Brigade, and went so far as to keep his own personal uniform hanging in the Chandos Street fire station by Charing Cross so that he could attend some of the more important fires!

In 1904 the organisation's name was changed to "The London Fire Brigade" and, gradually, more and more innovations came to be introduced. There were motor vehicles, of course, which in 1921 ousted the long-established horse for good and all.

During the First World War, the Brigade lost many men to the armed services. But when air-raids began (they were light enough, compared to those in the last war) men still serving in the Brigade were exempted from call-up.

It was between the wars that our Fire Brigade really began to modernise into the form we know it today. Larger, enclosed machines came into use—which meant fewer accidents caused when firemen fell off the engines! New, faster fireboats for

Fireman fight to bring a blaze under control, hampered by falling material.

the river service made their appearance, and the existing headquarters building went up on the Albert Embankment by Lambeth Bridge. Working hours were shortened for the firemen's shifts, and the old brass helmet was replaced by a much stronger cork one.

When the Second World War broke out, the Government ordered the recruitment of an Auxiliary Fire Service, so that the existing brigade could be strengthened to meet the incessant emergencies that arose during the bombing. Auxiliaries and regulars together did a wonderful job during the flaming days of the Blitz and Churchill, in one of his famous speeches, dubbed them "the heroes with grimy faces".

As the war continued, the fire services of the whole country were banded together under the title "National Fire Service", and it wasn't until 1948 that they were reassembled into separate bodies to come under individual county council control.

The London Fire Brigade of today came into being in 1965, with the creation of the Greater London Council. It serves an area of some six hundred and twenty square miles, and is responsible for the protection from fire of around eight million people!

Firemen serving with the Brigade, when they're not out answering emergency calls (there were nearly sixty-six thousand of them in 1968) spend a great deal of their time keeping physically fit. They have to be in peak condition to carry out the dangerous and difficult tasks that arise during the control of any fire. The firemen also carry out daily drills with the many types of equipment that are the tools of his trade, so that he can use them quickly and efficiently.

Again, the men of the Brigade have to keep up-to-date with the latest fire-fighting methods and with building materials and techniques, so that they can work out how fires are likely to behave. They must get to know their 'ground'—their station areas—like the backs of their hands. In addition, they must be prepared to carry out routine hydrant inspections and tests, and make visits to factories and other places to test fire equipment and make periodic checks on fire prevention methods.

With an average of seventy fires a day to handle, you wouldn't expect that the London Fire Brigade has much time for anything else. Yet the service handles around ten thousand special service calls a year in addition. Attendance at road, rail and aircraft crashes, the rescue of people trapped in tunnels, lifts and sewers, coping with flooded premises . . . all these are 'special services'. These jobs usually go to specially trained crews with equipment designed to deal with almost any emergency.

The ever patient fireman will turn out at any time of the day or night to tackle fire. He will extract people trapped in machinery, and cheerfully recover your cat from a high tree. If you're daft enough to poke your head through the park railings and get it stuck, it'll be a fireman who comes to get it out again. But there *is* one thing that's guaranteed to take the smile off even a fireman's face, and that's when he's called out on a false alarm by some idiot with warped ideas of a practical joke. The firemen term these calls "malicious", and incredible though it seems, there are over ten thousand of them every year! One can only hope that it will be the joker's own house that burns down while the fire engine is away answering his false alarm! ■

One of the modern appliances used by the London Fire Brigade in their fight to protect eight million people from fire hazards.

ARCTIC WALK

At first thought, you might imagine it would be easy. After all, we've most of us seen pictures of the North Pole and the vast ice-cap on top of the world. Solid enough? Apart from the cold, what's to stop anyone travelling across it? The truth is that, unlike the South Polar regions of Antarctica, the northern ice-mass isn't founded on land. It's just frozen water, always on the move, affected by the changing seasons and often breaking up into terrifying pressure-ridges and 'leads' of open sea. It wasn't until 1969 that men first made a surface crossing of the frozen Arctic . . . a journey that had long been considered by experts to be impossible. . . .

Tony Bastable

"MAN HAS CROSSED all the deserts, climbed the highest mountains, made his first cautious probes into the oceans and into space, and only one pioneer journey is left to him on the surface of the earth."

The words were Wally Herbert's, and the challenge in them was enough to take him through ten years of dreaming, scheming, planning and reconnaissance before that historic day—February 21st, 1968—when he set out with three companions to make the epic journey from Alaska to Spitzbergen.

They called themselves the British Trans-Arctic Expedition. Wally Herbert, Allan Gill, Fritz Koerner and Kenneth Hedges. Scientists, explorers, gamblers who staked their lives and their experience for the prize of achievement.

They set out from Point Barrow, at the northern edge of Alaska, with forty Greenland Huskies in ten-dog teams and seventy thousand pounds of food, fuel and equipment. Before them lay a measured linear distance of almost two thousand miles. Yet they had estimated that the drifting of the ice upon which they would be travelling would increase their actual journey to something like three thousand eight hundred.

An incredible distance . . . so why do it with dogs? Why not copy others who had tried and failed, and use motorised sledges? The simple answer lay in the fact that dogs are more reliable. They haven't the machine's irritating tendency to break down.

They're more nimble, and aren't as likely to fall down ice fissures that open up with disturbingly little warning. Also, in the event of dire emergency, they can be eaten!

Huddled into their wolfskin parkas, the four men set off. By sundown that first day they had travelled only five miles, and the lights of Barrow Point were still in sight behind them. But they were on sea-ice, and their whole attention was focused on the critical crossing of a fractured zone North of Barrow. The going was diabolically hard, and the teams had to hack a way through a chaotic jumble of blocks that looked as though they'd been scattered haphazardly by some maniac giant.

The route was treacherous and deceptive. Time and again Herbert and his companions had to retrace their steps. Time and again a hopeful trail came to nothing against massive pressure walls—great ridges of ice thrown up by the collision of ice floes. There was initial trouble with the dogs. One had been killed by the others in a snarling quarrel.

They camped, their two tents small and insignificant in a wild landscape whose constant movement was ceaselessly advertised by a cacophony of nerve-grating screeches and ominous rumblings. On the

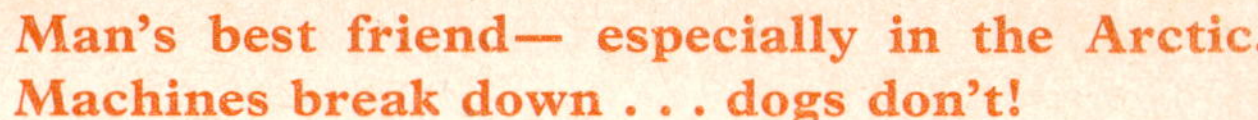

Man's best friend— especially in the Arctic. Machines break down . . . dogs don't!

eighth night, they'd become so used to the noise that, if Wally Herbert hadn't happened to step outside his tent for a moment, nobody would have been aware that the floe on which they were based was breaking up! Two massive splits had appeared on each side of the camp, and even as they rushed to strike camp and hitch up the dogs, two more cracks appeared at right-angles to the others, cutting them off on a floating island of ice no more than eighty yards by sixty—an ice-pan that threatened to shatter to smaller fragments at any moment!

It was a tense moment . . . the first of many. And the dogs had to be forced to leap a treacherous 'lead' of open sea to safer ice.

They reached a likely spot and re-pitched. But the whole night had to be spent on total guard, and the spotter aircraft that flew over them reported their position as 'precarious'.

It was thanks to their watchdog pilots that Wally and his friends were kept informed of the state of the ice ahead. They were also checked out for position, and often the news was unfavourable and discouraging. In those early February days, they often found themselves carried far off course by the drifting pack, so that their progress towards the North Pole, and to Spitzbergen beyond, was frequently cancelled out.

They pressed on . . . over miles of ground-up mush-ice knit together by a pitifully thin film of freezing water. Luckily, the weather was calm, for the effect of a high wind would have been to move the surrounding floes and crush their slim foothold to nothing.

It was early April before the expedition got clear of the dangerous area of coastal currents and reached safer, more predictable drifts. By the time they had their first re-supply air-drop from the Royal Canadian Air Force on May 10th, they had been carried far to the West, and although they had covered an actual route distance of nine hundred miles, they were depressingly out of schedule and a long, long way from their goal. Worse, their sledges were beginning to suffer, and they had had to make hasty repairs to split runners and fractured handlebars. Snow had fallen, and continued to fall. The cracks and fissures that lay like traps in the ice had been covered, and the weather was sapping their strength. Wally Herbert recorded dismally that they were making an average of two miles a day!

Four months out, the four men began to think of pitching their summer camp. There wasn't much hope of progressing any farther that season, for the old floes were splitting, and black sea-pools were spreading all around them.

In July, they made their two-month permanent home on a likely floe, their only encouraging thought being the knowledge that they had sledged farther from land over the polar ice than any other men before them. Their notebooks were already bulging with data recording floe thicknesses, the types and ages of ice, the weather, wild life. Now they built themselves a marquee out of parachutes that had been used in the summer air-drop, made themselves crude furniture out of packing crates, and began the long series of scientific tests on their surroundings and their survival equipment. They shot a polar bear that had wandered into their camp (they called it "Meltville"—or rather, the home press did). They fixed the sledges and made new dog traces, and they took photographs. Ken Hedges, wearing a special Neoprene wet-suit, even dived below the surface of an open lead to take pictures of the sub-surface of ice-floes for Fritz Koerner.

There were bears and seals around, not that the expedition needed them for food. The dogs liked them, but there was still the concentrate of whale meat, dried yeast, skimmed milk powder, maize starch, beef dripping and vitamins that had been specially supplied for the trip.

During the summer, Wally Herbert concentrated on writing. In addition he had to work the hand generator for the necessary power to transmit his articles by radio. Ken was largely responsible for research on the clothing. Allan's main job was navigation . . . and his sunshots confirmed a welcome drift almost due north. Fritz was always busy with his complex mass of scientific apparatus.

From summer camp, the expedition had to make a rapid move into another for the winter. The floe they were already on was quite unsuitable for, by September, it had moved too far east to pick up the trans-polar drift stream that would carry it towards the Pole.

On September 4th, they set off again . . . across tricky, ice-sheeted pools, around terrible chasms half-hidden by crystalline snow. Through knee-deep channels of slush. Progress was painfully slow, and after only a few days, what might have turned out to be disaster happened! Allan Gill hurt his back while trying to manhandle his stuck sledge!

It was clear he'd either slipped a disc or sustained a bad muscle-strain, and there began a long radio argument with the expedition's sponsors to determine whether or not he would be airlifted out. It was only the weather conditions that prevented this actually happening, but luckily, Gill made a recovery, and the trouble never returned.

In late September, they chose the floe for their winter quarters and built a permanent hut. Once the floor had been laid, the structure went up in about nine hours . . . a cylindrical 'home' equivalent to a fairly small room in a suburban house. The place was heated by a Coleman stove, burning kerosene, which kept a fairly constant living temperature of sixty degrees fahrenheit . . . quite comfortable, thank you. The floor was bare, so that any ice that formed there could easily be got rid of, and each man had a 'corner' of the accommodation which he had to furnish himself with packing-case wood.

They took turns with the cooking, and in four weeks, had settled in nicely to a workable routine. There were five depots of fuel and food scattered on the mile-wide floe, and the dogs were tethered down-wind of a sacred, inviolable area where Fritz Koerner set up his equipment for meteorological study.

Their research programme ran again smoothly . . . until one day in October when a split cleft their floe down the middle! Wally Herbert reckoned the cause may have been the physical jerks practised by the expedition members outside the hut as a daily routine! Moving camp became an

The British Trans-Arctic Expedition— left to right, Wally Herbert, Ken Hedges, Fritz Koerner and Allan Gill.

urgent necessity, and although the struggle cost them about a month's work, they made it without loss in only a few days.

Wally and his companions kept their camp meticulously neat and tidy. The debris that accumulated as they ate their way through their stores was stacked in piles well away from the hut. There were two reasons. Dumps attract snow and create drifts, and they didn't want their home buried. Additionally, it was possible that their camp might be taken over by geological personnel flown out to continue research, and the members of the British Trans-Arctic Expedition didn't want to hand over the place looking like a pigsty! In fact, the hut wasn't taken over, for on the morning of February 24th—over a year since the expedition had started—the winter floe began breaking up, and the whole team had to drop everything and get away before the ice broke to bits and ditched them!

The evacuation was hectic. The break-up had taken them by surprise, and it was only by using floating pans of ice as rafts that they managed to get everything to safety!

They were three hundred and twenty-two statute miles from the Pole, and now their route lay across ice criss-crossed with fissures and leads, over pressure-fields where ridges of packed up, towering ice came crumbling towards them to the tune of banshee screeching and cracking. Then Allan's sledge gave up, and shortly afterwards, the other three followed suit. And these were replacement sledges that had already taken the place of the first four used by the party!

The men made repairs to the splits in the runners, caused by brittleness of the wood due to the sub-zero temperatures, and miraculously, the repairs lasted for the rest of the journey. Metal plates, bolts and raw-hide lashings had averted disaster!

The temperature was only one problem.

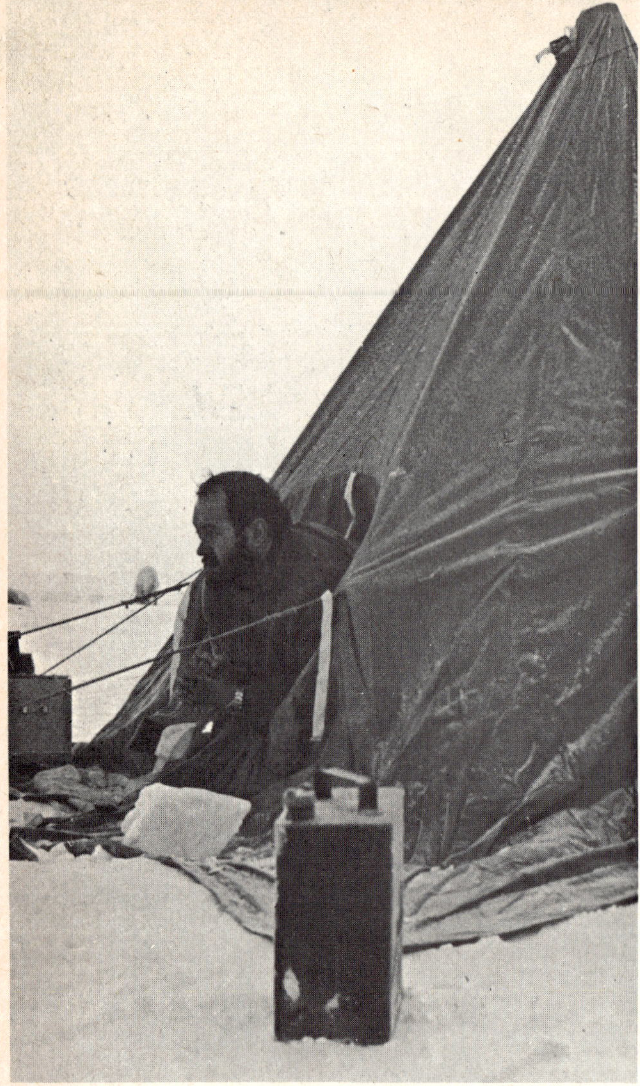

Wally Herbert—on constant watch against the break-up of the polar ice . . .

Every time they pitched camp, they had to make an 'ice-hole'—actually two holes connected by a short tunnel, so that a rope could be passed through for tethering the dog teams. Their mitts would ice up in the shape of a clenched fist so that they couldn't get them off or on without thawing.

But soon, conditions began to get better. The weather improved, and so did the surface over which they were travelling. They began to find 'sastrugi'—packed, wind-polished snow formed in ridges rather like a ploughed field. It doesn't sound like it, but it's an ideal floor for sledging. From time to time, the going was so good that, for the first time, the dog teams were actually able to break into a gallop, and the spirits of the expedition members began to rise.

It was on Easter Sunday 1969 that they reached the North Pole . . . the first Britons ever to do so. There, they experienced the unique sensation of standing on a spot where the terms North, East and West simply do not exist, and every direction points South!

But they had only sixty days left to complete their transarctic programme. Sixty days in which to cover a minimum of six hundred nautical miles. Wally Herbert was worried. They needed supplementary rations. They had to lighten their gear.

The expedition got their supplies—although a break in radio contact made the situation look desperate for a while. There was talk in the home press that the expedition was lost, and in dire peril of perishing on the ice without food or fuel.

And perils there were, of course. The going was just as trying as it ever had been, and there was a narrow escape for Allan Gill when a floe broke up underneath him. It was only by desperate action on the part of the team that he wasn't lost along with his sledge and dogs.

On May 10th, they reached the point on their route at which they were to turn and head for land. Their target was Phipps Island, and they sighted it on the 23rd. The day was perfect . . . yet the land that was so near was at the same time far away. They couldn't exactly rush across and jump on it. Besides the problems of route, there were polar bears, too . . . a lot of them. The creatures were proving a real menace, and seemed utterly fearless. The only way to get rid of them was to shoot them, and even this was becoming tricky, for ammunition was running out. The expedition members tried throwing ice-axes to scare them off. It didn't work. One of them threw a boot, which the bear in question promptly chewed to shreds.

But despite the bears, and despite a tense moment when Wally's sledge overturned and almost ruined precious camera equipment in a melt-pool, the expedition reached the end of the floe separating them from their target. Unfortunately, there was a huge stretch of water and mush-ice between, and they had to travel the edge in ever-mounting frustration, looking for a place to get across.

They didn't make it. The floe drifted, and they had to alter their objective to the smaller, granite upthrust known as Little Blackboard Island. Even then, they looked in danger of a disappointing ultimate failure, but two members of the party, Allan and Ken, risked a dash across incredibly treacherous thin ice to claim a couple of rock samples and set the seal of success on the efforts of the British Trans-Arctic Expedition.

It only remained to tell the world, and to await helicopter pick-up that would ferry them to HMS Endurance. It was May 29th, and Wally, Allan, Ken and Fritz had come three thousand, six hundred and twenty miles across the top of the world from Point Barrow, Alaska. They had satisfied the appeal of the trip . . . the appeal that, in Wally Herbert's own words, consisted of "the bigness of it. The bigness in time, the bigness in distance, the bigness as a challenge—a challenge of human endurance."

MEET THE HUSKY PUPS

AREN'T THEY GORGEOUS? The pups, we mean . . . although Susan's okay too, of course!

They're six-week-old huskies, and their mother and father were Eskimo Nell and Apple Dog, two of the sledge-dogs who made the British Trans-Arctic Expedition journey with Wally Herbert and his colleagues.

They were all born in quarantine, these pups, and they've all got new owners here in Britain. A real bundle of fun, they're absolutely fearless. You should have seen them in the studio, trying to eat the fake snow, and rushing to investigate when one of the light bulbs exploded!

There are a hundred or so huskies in this country, and they have unusual habits like trying to bury their food as though they're still living in the ice and snow! They need lots of exercise, and if more than one is kept, there has to be a 'boss'—just like there is in any polar dog-team!

Murgatroyd's Mind-Bogglers! ②

Here's Murgatroyd back with some more posers, just in case your mind feels like a bit more boggling! Take a look at the pictures on this page and see if you can guess what they are!

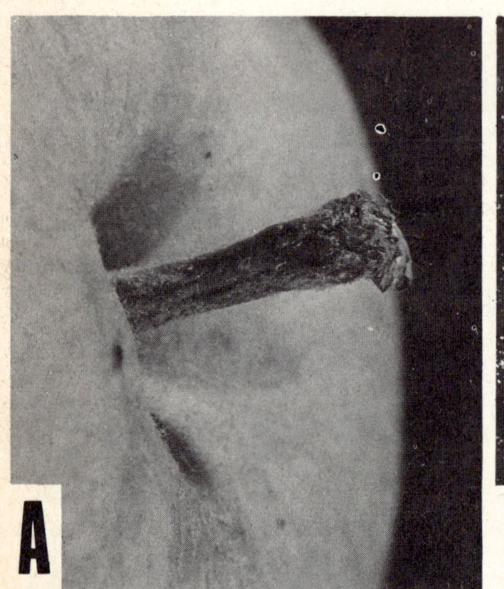

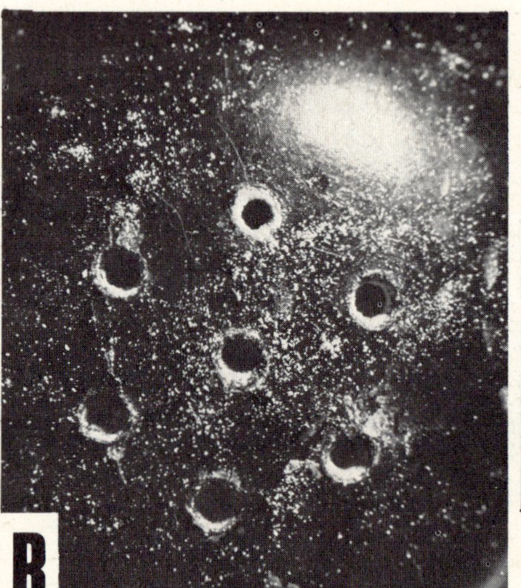

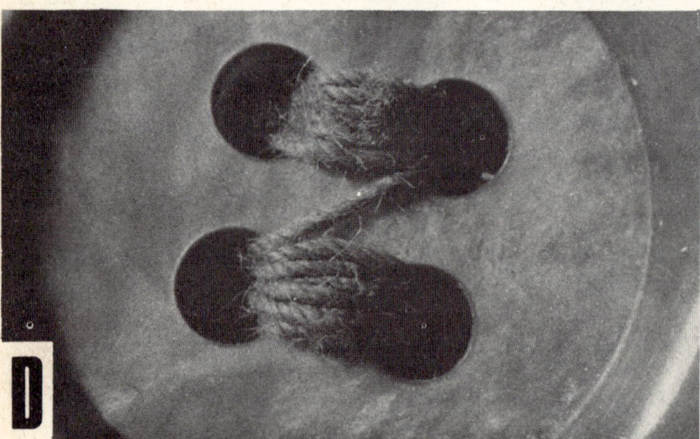

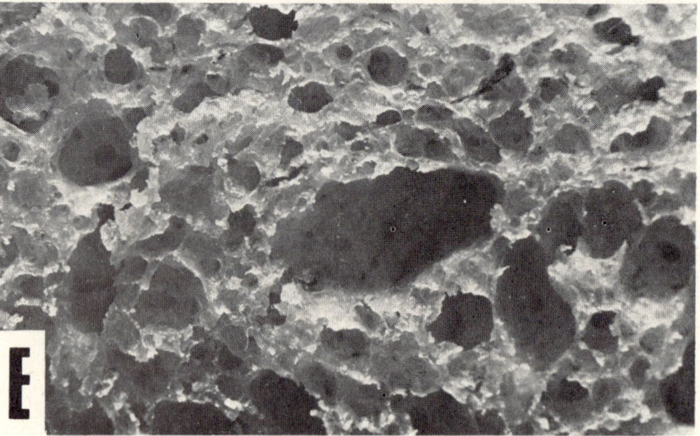

EVER BEEN HAD?

It's possible to have a perfectly correct, meaningful sentence in English, with the word 'had' appearing *eleven* consecutive times! Sounds impossible, doesn't it . . . but you'll see the way on page 75 if you're stumped!

WHO IS IT?

Picture a man standing looking at a painted portrait. He says to himself: "Brothers and sisters have I none, but that man's father is my father's son." What is the relationship of the man in the portrait to the man looking at it?

IT'S A ROCKY, FOSSILISED WORLD!

The impression of an ancient palm-leaf in sedimentary rock, found at Bournemouth.

Can you tell Gneiss from Schist? It's dead easy, really. Gneiss (you pronounce it like 'nice') is a chunk of rock in which minerals are laid down in thick light-and-dark layers. Schist, on the other hand, has the minerals arranged in thin, flaky layers!

The story of things like Gneiss and Schist goes back thousands of millions of years, when the earth was just a mass of molten rock. As it cooled, lots of these rocks became solid. Some were on the surface, to be broken down by the weather. Others, inside the earth, were compressed, twisted, forced about and altered by heat. Many of them were thrust into the air by underground volcanic activity . . . and all the time, various substances within them were being chemically changed into what we now term minerals.

Rocks and minerals have all found their uses with mankind. Granite, marble, slate and limestone in building, chalk for cement, crystalline gemstones for jewellery, salt for preserving and flavouring, coal for burning, and so on and so on.

You don't have to be a miner to find examples of interesting rocks and minerals. They're all around us. We walk on them, kick them, tip-toe over them on pebbly beaches, and even turn them up in scores every time we dig the garden. The almost endless varieties make a marvellous collection, and if they're collected in small pieces, they can be used to build up glorious mosaic pictures on glued boards, or stuck in patterns on otherwise dull boxes.

If you go looking for them, whether it be up in the Scottish Highlands or down on Brighton Beach, over on the Norfolk coast or deep in the Welsh mountains, all you really need is a stout knapsack and a small hammer. The rest is merely a matter of using your eyes.

Explaining and illustrating all the various

This fossil lobster shows how ancient remains can be turned to stone and buried in rock. You have to break open large stones to find them.

finds you can pick up would fill a small book at the very least . . . and your local library is bound to have several such volumes to help you identify whatever you come across. But here's a general guide to some of the more interesting samples to be found in Britain.

Selenite crystals are beautiful, transparent pieces of calcium sulphate, like pendant-drop gems. They were formed in clay, and can be found on the beaches of North Kent. They look very well in an arrangement alongside Sussex Marble, which is a limestone occurring in the southern counties, composed of millions of the crushed shells of pond-snails which were laid down one hundred and thirty million years ago in the lakes of South-East England. You can see the shapes of these tiny shells very clearly, and the stone itself was a favourite decoration in medieval churches.

Fossil wood, which looks just like bits of tree, but is white and absolutely stony, can be found in the cliffs of Lulworth Cove, Dorset, and fossil coral, a porous-looking, pitted rock found in limestones near Oxford, actually comes from warm seas that once covered the area!

Hertfordshire puddingstone is a little younger. It's only about fifty million years old, and can be found all over the Chilterns. It looks like a sort of pudding, made of compacted flints and pebbles, cemented by minerals into an extremely hard rock.

It's worth breaking open any large pebbles you find on beaches, by the way. Lots of them have fossils inside, and reveal the curious shapes of long-extinct sea-creatures.

Alabaster can be found in the red marl cliffs in South-West England and Wales, and is a pink or white soft, crystalline mineral. Look for Celestine crystal there too—a clear mineral that yields the metal strontium. You may find the ores of zinc and lead, called Blende and Galena. They're very much alike, and are both almost the colour of lead itself. They are, of course, crystalline. There's Barytes, too . . . a source of barium. It feels decidedly heavy, and can come in all sorts of colours.

Easier to recognise is Cornish Cassiterite—the principal source of tin. It often appears as streaks and bits in lumps of glittering quartz, and may be accompanied by yellow traces of copper pyrites.

Pyrites of copper is very often mistaken for gold, because it looks so brassy. You can't walk along the rocky bed of a highland

A fossil ammonite, found in Folkestone. Ammonites are the shells of extinct creatures, some of them up to 180 million years old.

stream without noticing it winking up at you in the sunlight. The stones there are sometimes so thick with it that you can feel positively rich with a lump of it in your hand! It isn't at all precious though, and it's generally known as 'fool's gold'.

Another attractive rock, found near The Lizard, is Serpentine. Normally green and red, Serpentine is a silicate, and one form of it comes as grey, silky fibres that are more like material than rock. In this form it is collected and spun into yarn to make fireproof asbestos.

Sometimes the shapes of rocks will help identify them, like the 'cannonball' concretions in the limestone of Durham. These are masses of tightly-packed, rocky balls, and are some 250 million years old. Then there's the iron ore, Haematite, of Barrow in Furness—called kidney-stone because that's exactly what it looks like.

Many rocks, like granite, are mixtures of minerals. Granite is composed of glassy quartz, white felspar and black biotite mica, for example, which gives it a mottled, silvery appearance.

Other minerals are pure, and occur as gemstones, precious or semi-precious, of which the latter aren't so hard to find as you'd think. You often see holidaymakers in the Highlands of Scotland making diligent searches among the screes and hillsides in the hope of picking up Agate, Garnet or Jasper. Then again, there's Amber, found on the beaches of Norfolk. But in fact, Amber is not a stone it is the fossilised sap of ancient pine trees.

Fossil Brachiopods, creatures from long forgotton seas that once covered Britain. Some of these were found in Derbyshire.

Speaking of fossils, you can make quite a collection of them alone. They aren't hard to come by, and fall into two main categories. First, there are fossils which have been preserved intact; the petrified remains (usually shells or bones) of creatures that died millions of years ago. Then, there are fossil impressions, where the outlines of creatures, or of leaves, have been impressed into rocks that formed on top of them. Almost all fossils come from sedimentary rocks, formed by layers of silt. They are never found in igneous rocks, which have been formed by volcanic process. The heat involved would have destroyed any trace of a living creature at once.

One final point about collecting. Whenever you find anything of interest, mark it clearly so that you can identify it later, and make a note of exactly where you found it. If you do this, you'll have a much better chance of discovering exactly what it is when you come to checking in the local library books!

HOW MINERAL VEINS ARE FORMED
Magma, or molten rock, cools when it forces its way up to and out of the earth's crust, becoming igneous rock. Liquids rich in dissolved minerals, carried with this magma, cool to form seams or veins, mineral ores crystallis-ing out,

TASTY

What tastes better than goodies you've made yourself? Nothing! But the trouble with kitchen do-it-yourself is that fingers have a knack of getting burned no matter how careful you are. Well, here are some simple recipes that call for no cooking at all, so there's positively no chance of ending up with a burnt offering.

A-ORANGE COCONUTS

$\frac{1}{2}$ cup condensed milk; 2 teasp. orange juice; 2 teaspoon orange rind, grated; $2\frac{1}{2}$ cups icing sugar; shredded coconut.

Mix orange juice and rind with the milk and add the icing sugar gradually, mixing well. Take teaspoonfuls of the mixture and drop into the coconut, rolling into balls. Place on greaseproof paper on a tray and finally pop them into the fridge to chill.

B-CHOCOLATE COCONUT ROCKS

$\frac{1}{2}$ lb icing sugar; 1 egg white; 2 tablespoons cocoa; $\frac{3}{4}$ lb desiccated coconut.

Mix all the dry ingredients together in a bowl and then make into a stiff paste with the egg white. Keep on stirring until it is thoroughly mixed, then divide into rough little lumps, using two forks. Leave to get thoroughly dry.

C-TROPICAL TRUFFLES

$\frac{1}{4}$ lb butter; $\frac{1}{2}$ lb milk chocolate, grated fine; 6 oz icing sugar; 1 teaspoon coffee essence; drinking chocolate powder.

Cream icing sugar and butter together, add coffee essence and chocolate and keep beating until firm. Leave for an hour, shape into balls and roll in chocolate powder.

TREATS and no cooking!

D-MARZIPAN FLOWERS

½ lb icing sugar; ¼ lb ground almonds; 1 beaten egg; few drops of almond essence and colouring; crystallised flowers to decorate.

Mix almonds and sugar together with egg, adding gradually and keeping the paste stiff. Add essence and colouring and knead smooth. Pinch off bits of the paste and make into little rolls, decorate.

E-COFFEE KINGS

1 lb icing sugar; the whites of 2 eggs; 1 teaspoon coffee essence; shelled walnuts.

Put the egg whites into a bowl and slowly mix in the icing sugar, whisking the mixture all the time. Add the coffee essence and keep whisking until the mixture is stiff. Roll into little balls and place greaseproof paper dusted with icing sugar. Top each sweet with half a walnut and leave to set.

F-FRUIT FLUFF

Two 4½ oz cans strained raspberry and apple baby food; 1 egg white, whipped stiffly; ½ pint double cream, whipped; chocolate vermicelli.

Fold the egg white and the cream together and blend the cans of raspberry and apple into the mixture. Spoon into jelly glasses and top off with a scatter of chocolate vermicelli. (This recipe makes enough for four.)

G-BANANA SHAKE

1 pint cold milk (from the fridge); 2 ripe bananas, well mashed; 1 small brickette vanilla ice cream, cubed.

Put all the ingredients together into a large bowl and whisk them with a rotary beater until thoroughly blended and foamy. Serve in tall glasses.

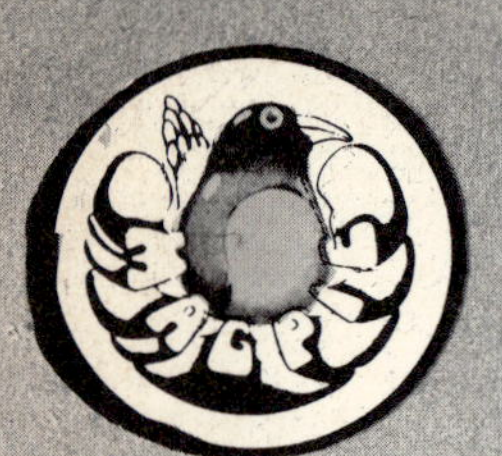

PENCIL AND

There's nothing like a simple game for two with a pencil and paper if it's rainy outside and you're feeling bored. You can get a lot of fun out of simple noughts-and-crosses, but why not go one better and try one of these instead?

HANGMAN

Take it in turns to be challenger and competitor. The first challenger thinks of a well-known phrase or saying—let's take, just as an example, 'More haste, less speed'. He marks the paper with dashes to represent each letter, like this:

– – – – – – – – – – – – – – – – – –

Now, the competitor chooses any letter he likes. Suppose he picks a 'T'. The challenger writes a 'T' where it appears in the phrase, like this:

– – – – – – – T –, – – – – – – – – –

If the competitor had chosen 'E', he would have had even more letters marked in:

– – – E – – – – E, – E – – – – E E –

But, if he'd chosen a 'W', which doesn't appear in the phrase at all, the challenger would have drawn the first line of the drawing known as a 'hangman'. You can see a completed 'hangman' below, made up of separate lines. Each line is added for every wrong guess the competitor makes. The idea is for the competitor to puzzle out the phrase before the 'hangman' is finished . . . and of course, the longer the phrase chosen, the better the fun!

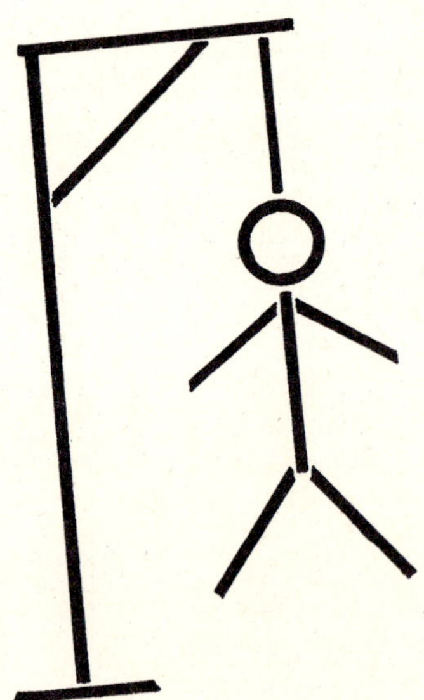

A completed 'hangman' showing each separate stroke to be made.

PAPER GAMES

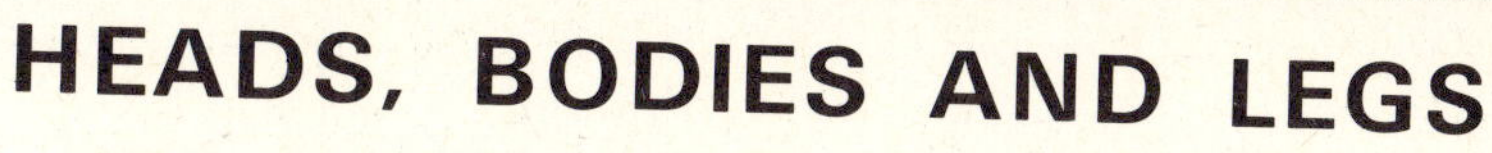

HEADS, BODIES AND LEGS

This isn't a competitive game, it's just an excuse for some fun! First of all, you have to fold a piece of paper into three (1). The first player draws a ridiculous, grotesque head . . . it can be the head of a human, a clown, an animal, a robot, a prehistoric monster . . . anything he likes. He runs the neck down over the first fold, as in sketch (2), and hands it to the next player—who *mustn't* be allowed to see the drawn head! This player adds any sort of crazy body he likes, indicates the legs, and passes the paper on, folded over again so that whoever has to draw the legs can't see the body. The last person draws ridiculous legs, with incredible feet, and declares the drawing to be finished. Then the paper is opened out and shown round . . . and the results always raise a laugh!

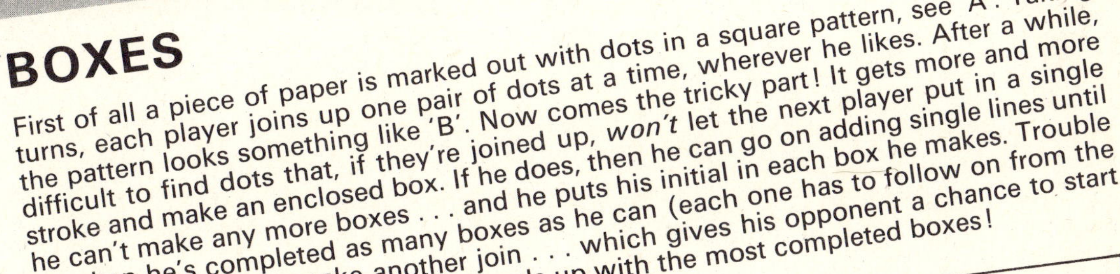

BOXES

First of all a piece of paper is marked out with dots in a square pattern, see 'A'. Taking turns, each player joins up one pair of dots at a time, wherever he likes. After a while, the pattern looks something like 'B'. Now comes the tricky part! It gets more and more difficult to find dots that, if they're joined up, *won't* let the next player put in a single stroke and make an enclosed box. If he does, then he can go on adding single lines until he can't make any more boxes . . . and he puts his initial in each box he makes. Trouble is, when he's completed as many boxes as he can (each one has to follow on from the last) he's still got to make another join . . . which gives his opponent a chance to start boxing! The winner is the one who ends up with the most completed boxes!

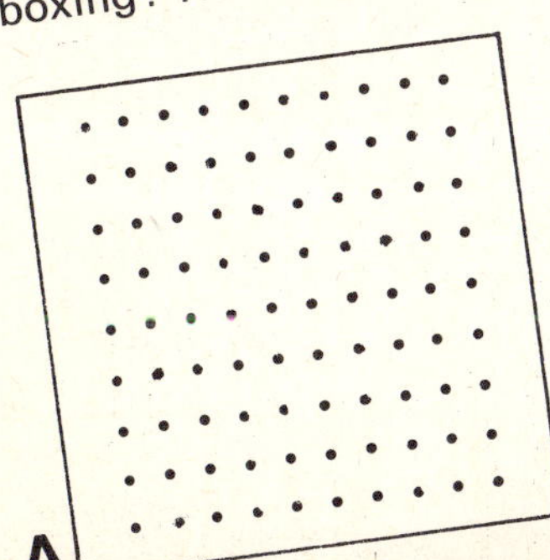

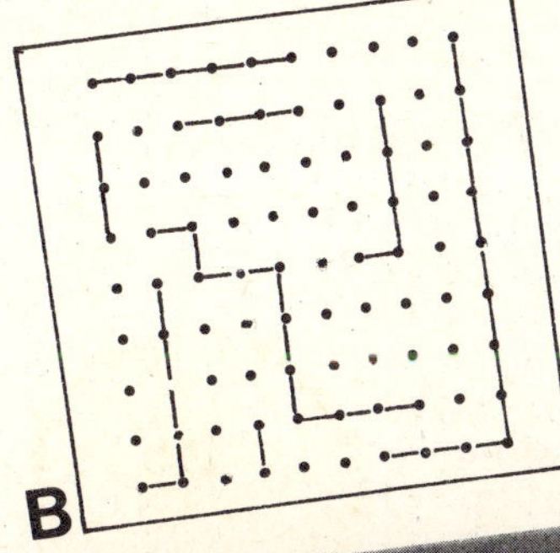

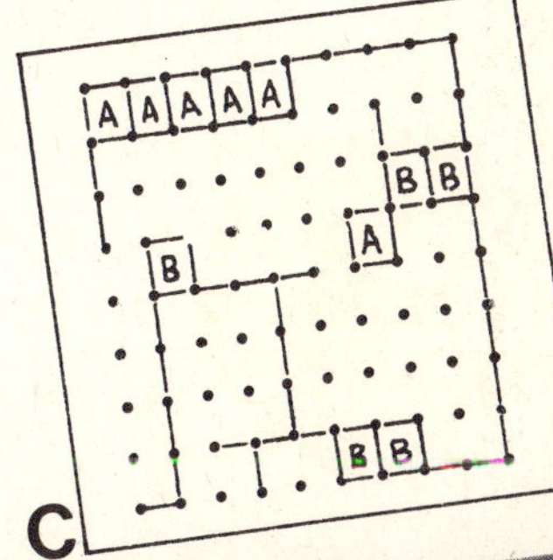

Bread. What is it? Flour and water? A little yeast? You could say that, and think no more about it. But it's worth looking into, this daily slice that we take so much for granted. After all, the average person in Britain—you and me—eats twice his own weight in bread every year!

Pete Brady

OUR

IT MUST HAVE been some time in the Stone Age that people stopped stuffing their mouths with the seeds of grasses that grew around their caves and decided they could do something better.

We don't know exactly where, when, or who . . . but someone, some genius with a name like Ug or Og or Gnnnr, thought of crushing the seeds and making a paste of their floury powder. He, with the help of his wife, who set the mixture to cook on hot stones, became the world's first ever baker.

The ancient Egyptians were perhaps the first to recognise the value of bread as a food. Termed 'the bread eaters' by other races of their time, the subjects of the Pharaohs had the whole thing beautifully organised, ploughing and sowing and reaping the harvest most efficiently.

Bread-making was fairly primitive, though. Slaves trod the dough barefoot in great vats, and spices always had to be added to give the loaves some flavour.

Nowadays, the making of bread is a major and extremely vital industry, involving all the techniques of automation, and a far cry from the small bakehouse production of a mere thirty years ago.

It all starts in the wheatfields of the world. In Canada, Australia, The Argentine. In India, Russia, and here in Great Britain. All of these wheats are different. That is, they have their own characteristics. For example, Canadian wheat is termed 'hard', and its strength makes a bold and attractive loaf. Argentine and Indian wheats are renowned for their flavour, and Australian wheat makes exceptionally white flour.

It's the job of the buyers who obtain wheat for the big milling companies to make sure that they buy in the right quantities of the various types, so that a first-class blend can be obtained.

Wheat arrives at the mills, often by large ocean tankers. The wheat is sucked from the holds with huge machines rather like giant

DAILY BREAD

vacuum cleaners, and is stored in silos . . . tall towers that are a recognisable feature of any flour mill.

The miller's first task is to clean the wheat and remove any impurities, and he does this by putting it through several washing, scouring and scrubbing machines.

Then comes the actual milling, where the wheat grain, or berry as it is sometimes called, is broken between sharp rollers. These split the grain, so that the husk can be removed in separators, which blow the husk away and leave the kernel, known as endosperm, and the tiny dark patch at one end which is wheatgerm.

More rollers tackle the kernels, and vibrating machines known as plansifters control the fineness of the finished flour. During the milling process, the wheatgerm is removed from the plain flour, partly because it spoils the colour, and partly because its richness in protein and fat makes it tend to go sour in storage. For certain breads, this extracted wheatgerm is cooked and returned to the flour later.

Finished flour is put into huge bins in the mill warehouse, from which it is piped into bulk tanker lorries that carry it direct to the bakeries.

When it arrives, the flour is sucked out of the tankers into the bakery silos, from which it is taken as required.

First, it is weighed out and sifted, and then transferred to the machines known as dough mixers, where it is mixed with water and yeast, and left to ferment. The contents of the mixers are then turned out into a divider, which accurately turns out raw loaves of the correct size and weight. These raw lumps of dough are shaped on a rotating conical moulder, and transferred to a machine called a 'prover', where they are circulated and left to rise. Then the pieces are put into tins automatically, and take another journey through the final prover before they pass into the ovens.

The loaves move through these ovens . . . which are long machines running the whole length of the bakery . . . by conveyor at controlled speed. The interior temperature of the ovens has to be very accurately set, and there are heat-resistant windows along the side to allow the bakers to watch their loaves' progress.

Finally, the baked loaves go to the cooler, and from there to the automatic slicers and

Flour leaves the mill. It's piped into these big bulk tanker lorries from huge storage bins above.

wrappers, where necessary. Ready to eat, the end product goes by van to the retail shops, and arrives nice and fresh on your table!

There are all sorts of loaves, of course. Brown and white, wholemeal (the flour used determines the type), cut and uncut, large and small. There are an enormous number of shapes, too—the bloomer, the farmhouse, the split, the flat tin. French sticks, viennas, and those highly decorative twists called 'chollas'—pronounced 'collars', by the way. These last are a survival from Roman times, when it was very fashionable to have bread baked in all sorts of fantastic designs. Caesar's bakers were used to turning out loaves in the shape of warships for the officers of the Imperial Navy, loaves like laurel wreaths for important senators, and loaves baked in interlocking rings for rich bridal couples.

Bread is much more than a pretty shape or a tasty crust. For example, the bread and flour eaten by the average person supplies 21% of the energy, 23% of the protein, 21% of the calcium, 25% of the iron, 27% of the vitamin B1, and 23% of the niacin of the body's daily requirements. In fact, nearly one quarter of the nourishment we need to keep us healthy! No wonder history has called the loaf of bread 'the staff of life'!

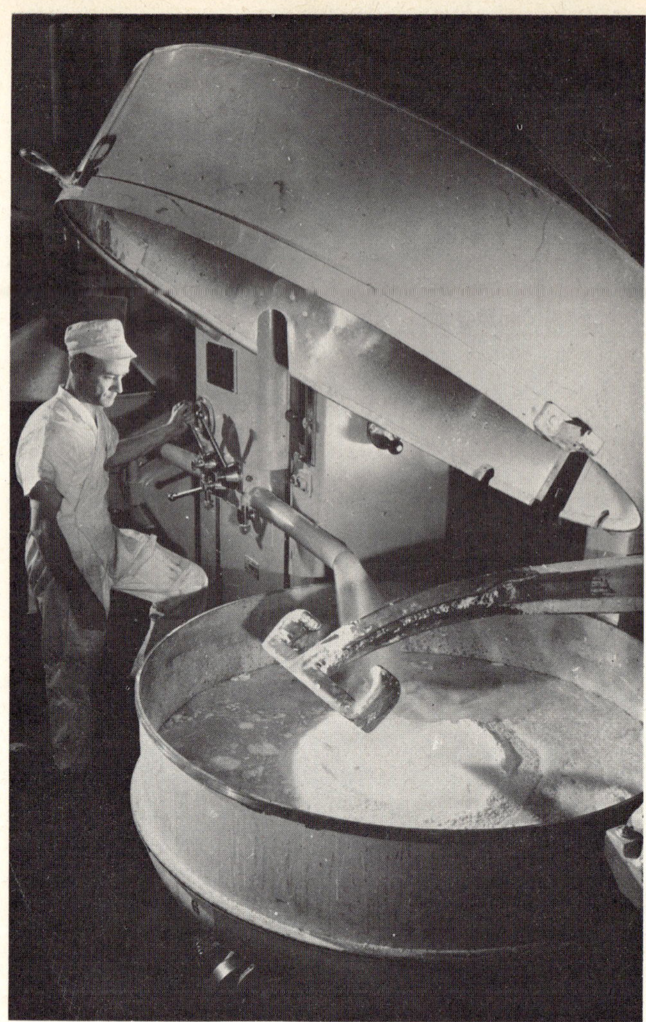

Dough in the mixer. The 'T' shaped arm does the mixing.

Freshly baked loaves coming out of the oven.

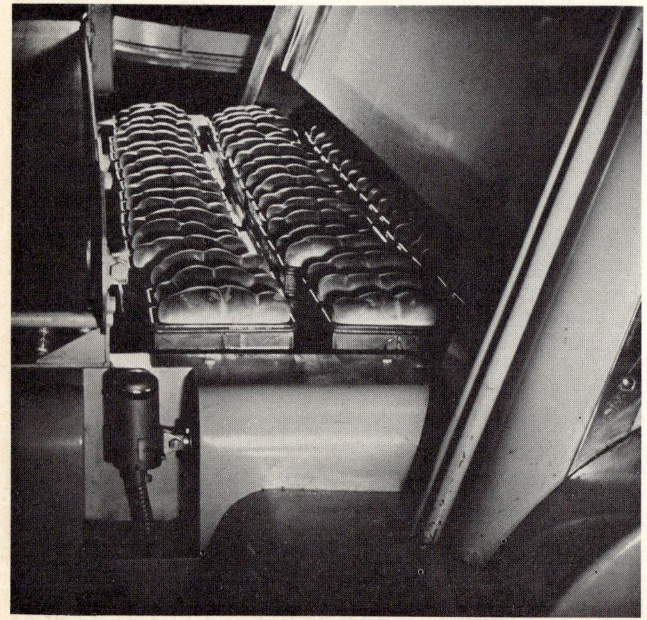

The finished product! Off the wrapping machines and onto the trolleys ready for the delivery vans!

OVER THE CHANNEL WITH THAMES MAGPIE

IN THE DECEMBER 1945 issue of the magazine 'Yachting World', the boat designer Arthur C. Robb had this to say about his Jenny Wren class motor-cruiser, a modified and slightly lengthened version of the Prize Winner in the 1938 design competition.

"Jenny Wren can be put to many uses. She could be used as a tender to a racing yacht, or shipped abroad for canal cruising on the Continent . . . "

Now, anyone who watches MAGPIE regularly on television, and anyone who read last year's Annual, will know that our own boat, **Thames Magpie**, is a modified Jenny Wren. And if Arthur C. Robb thought his cruiser design would have to be shipped across to the Continent, *we've* proved that he was being unnecessarily modest!

In July 1969, we took her across the English Channel under her own power, and she couldn't have behaved more reassuringly!

The Channel at Dover didn't look very inviting! Everything in the harbour was nice and calm, but the big cross-channel steamers weren't looking as smug as usual as they set out with their apprehensive passengers for the rough water beyond. There was an awful gale blowing, and the height of the seas were enough to make even hardened sailors swallow nervously!

Thames Magpie had lain there for two days before everyone decided that the sea had grown calm enough for the crossing. And it *still* looked rougher out there than we'd have liked!

Tony Bastable wasn't there . . . he had the bad luck to be ill at the time. But Susan Stranks and Pete Brady took their places in Thames Magpie beside the skipper, and the five-man camera team set themselves up on the specially-strengthened after portion of our boat, ready for the 'off'. All the documents had been cleared, both for Thames Magpie and for the escort vessel, crammed with the production staff, relief camera teams and engineers whose job was to bring our seafaring adventure back to you, the viewers.

Then we were away, cast off for'ard and aft, and heading for the troubled waters beyond the harbour moles!

"I don't like the look of it out there," said Pete . . . and he was well qualified to make the comment. Much of the time he'd spent in the West Indies he'd spent afloat, in everything from small outboard boats to two-masted inter-island schooners up to seventy feet in length! Far more reassuring craft than Thames Magpie with its waterline length of twenty-one feet, and its single mast with gunter mainsail and single jib! If you're wondering what a gunter is, by the way, it's simply a rig where the mainsail (the one that points rearward, or 'aft') is four-sided, the top edge secured to a pivoting 'gunter yard' forked against the mast. It's easier to show the rig in the illustration than to describe it in words!

JENNY WREN CLASS MOTOR CRUISER

Anyhow, Susan, bright and optimistic as ever, didn't seem to share Pete's misgivings, and sure enough, as soon as Thames Magpie hit the waves in open water, she had the rewarding sight of a surprised smile breaking out all over her fellow-presenter's face! "Hey, she's riding *beautifully*!"

With an easterly wind coming right at her, Thames Magpie's sails helped to stabilise her. You might think it odd that a boat can sail against the wind, but in fact the whole thing works in the same way as air pressure on the *top* of an aeroplane's wings keeps her up in the air. You see, with the sails well sheeted home (that's pulled tight, in landlubber language) the wind streams over the front surface and creates a sort of suction at the back, which pulls the boat along. Additionally, the new Stuart-Turner engine we'd had fitted helped her way through the water.

Of course, there was a certain amount of pitching, but as Pete explained, the smaller the boat, the more irregular the motion is, and therefore the less likelihood of seasickness.

It took five hours to cross the Channel to Calais, but gradually, the roughness of the sea disappeared until there was a flat calm! There was even time for Thames Magpie to come down to slow speed while Pete tried his hand at some fishing.

"I'd been on and on about catching something ever since we were in Dover," said Pete. "Because fishing is one of the pastimes I really enjoy. Naturally, I had to put up with everyone making the corny old jokes about old boots and bedsteads, but I'd taken no notice, and I brought my own tackle with me on the off chance. I fixed up a spinner with a two-pound weight on the end, and let it go. The weight had to be heavy, otherwise the spinner wouldn't have been able to sink enough, because of the speed we were making. Anyway, I felt some kind of shock on the line, and reeled in. First laugh for the doubting Thomases . . . the hook had disappeared! But I tried again, felt another shock, and pulled up a mackerel. I must say, I was rather proud of it, though it wouldn't have challenged any kind of fishing record! I'd have liked to have stopped and had another go, sinking and drawing feather lures . . . because where there's one mackerel, there's bound to be a whole lot more. But there just wasn't time, because we had a schedule to meet! I had to be content with my one catch."

Thames Magpie reached the French coast and put into Calais with no trouble at all. The crossing had been a copybook exercise. But her voyage wasn't over yet. Not by a long chalk.

From Calais, she was taken up the coast, and into the delta estuary of the Scheldt, where the vast network of Dutch rivers and canals begins, and the Maas, the Waal and the Lek empty their waters from Germany and France.

Under engine now, for bridges and locks present problems for the vessel under sail, Thames Magpie navigated the canals through to Amsterdam, and for two weeks, the presenters—all three of them, since Tony had recovered in time to join the others—spent their time seeing Western Holland.

"One of the most impressive trips was through Rotterdam Harbour," they all agreed. "The place is absolutely *enormous*! Words can't possibly describe it. You get big, big tankers . . . the largest in the world . . . coming down at speed. Just imagine the bow-wave and wash they leave in their wake! Poor old Thames Magpie was thrown around like a cork in the towering six-footers, but everyone loved it! It was just like being on a wild roller-coaster! Even small tugs, belting in and out of the harbour, set up fantastic washes, and there were times when several of these washes coincided, all from different directions!"

Dutch delicacy—smoked herring . . . "But it's not as good as the mackerel I caught", says Pete!

The presenters visited the historic cheese market at Alkmaar, which takes place every Friday morning, and is so important that a special train called the Kaas-express (Cheese-express) runs from Amsterdam and Rotterdam for the occasion.

They saw Amsterdam and the Hague, with its seaside resort of Scheveningen and its vast model city of Madurodam—built in honour of a young student, George Maduro, who died in a concentration camp during the last war.

"We travelled," said Pete, over areas that, incredible though it seemed, had once been totally under sea-water. Up and down canals that themselves were far below sea-level. How they got to be that way is part of another story, that Susan's going to introduce. All that's left for me to say is that, when we reluctantly left Holland, we had to fly back. After our happy fortnight with Thames Magpie, we'd have all preferred to sail, but there you are . . . they say all good things have to come to an end, and time just wasn't on our side!" ■

MAGPIE REPORT

MAGPIE LOOKS AT HOLLAND

There's a well-known expression, "God made the world, but the Dutch made Holland". One fifth of the country, occupied by more than half the population, actually lies below sea-level, and the map of Holland today is vastly different from a map drawn five centuries or so ago. While we were in Holland with Thames Magpie, I thought it would be a good idea to find out just how *these Dutchmen have battled with the sea for so many years, and I discovered that they're* still *battling . . . reclaiming more and more land to house their crowded population . . .*

Susan Stranks

THE WORD 'DYKE' means a ditch in Scotland and the far North of England. It means a kind of wall in the South. In Holland, where it's spelled 'dijk' it means an artificial, man-made barrier against the wild North Sea!

Keeping the sea from their low-lying land is nothing new to the people of The Netherlands. They built dykes and drained salt water from the fertile soil beneath as far back as the tenth century. These reclaimed areas, pumped dry and made suitable for agriculture, they called 'polders', and they still do.

They needed this extra land, not only for their own economy, but to reduce the long, winding areas of coastline that had to be defended against their enemies.

It wasn't until the beginning of the seventeenth century that the Dutch were able to turn their attention to the big lakes and marshes, for up until then, their efforts had had to be confined to small projects requiring only elementary technology. Then came the invention of the rotating turret windmill, which made it possible for the windwheels to be turned in any direction to catch the wind. Here in Britain, most of our windmills were used for the purpose of grinding corn into flour, but in Holland, the 'molen' drove pumps, specifically designed to drain the land.

It so happened that the rich merchants of Holland had made vast fortunes in the

East and West Indies during the seventeenth century. These men were able to finance the massive projects, and gradually, huge areas of land were reclaimed and sown with crops. The idea was to dam the sea with large dykes of clay, sand and rock, pump off as much of the sea-water as possible from the enclosed areas, and let the flushing action of the big European rivers clear the rest. The rivers were themselves enclosed and controlled by inner dykes, and transport and irrigation problems were solved by the construction of canals. Fresh water levels were regulated by 'locks'—familiar enough on the canals of our own country.

One of the biggest projects was the drainage of the 'Haarlemermeer'—the lake south of Amsterdam that occupied 47,000 acres, and which often menaced the Capital City in times of gale and storm. For this mammoth operation, which took place in the years of the mid-nineteenth century, steam-driven pumping stations were used for the first time, so beginning the gradual decline of the windmill. The bed of the Haarlem Lake is absolutely dry nowadays, of course—and looks very much like any other part of the flat country. But it's still 15 feet below sea-level, and any traveller who lands by plane at Amsterdam's Schiphol Airport can see a monument there that says so. The very name 'Schiphol' means ship-hole, and conjures up frightening pictures of Davy Jones's Locker, and the company of fish!

By far the most important step in the business of land reclamation was taken at the beginning of the twentieth century, when the decision was made to drain parts of the Zuyder Zee—the huge salt-water area that cut into the very middle of The Netherlands. The main part of the project involved the building of a dyke running from North Holland Province to Friesland . . . a distance of thirty kilometers—that's about eighteen miles for anyone who hasn't switched over to the metric system yet!

The construction of this barrier dam—known as the Afsluitdijk—began in 1927, and was completed five years later in 1932. First, soft layers of silt were dredged away from the sea-bed on the site of the dyke, and replaced with firmer sand. Then two parallel dams of boulder clay were erected on top of this foundation, and the space in between was filled with the core of the dyke. The outer surfaces were covered with brushwood mattresses, piled with rubble and strengthened with stone or concrete. Piles were driven in to strengthen the whole thing, and then began the construction of a highway along the top. Grass was sown on the banks of the dyke to prevent erosion by wind and weather, and then the drainage operations began on the enclosed water.

Pumping stations keep the enclosed land dry, and already, the huge polder of Eastern Flevoland is under cultivation, while work continues to drain two more polders—

This map shows the huge areas of recent Dutch land reclamation. 'A' is the dam that has made possible the draining of the old Zuyder Zee, and the blacked out areas in the South are those that will be reclaimed.

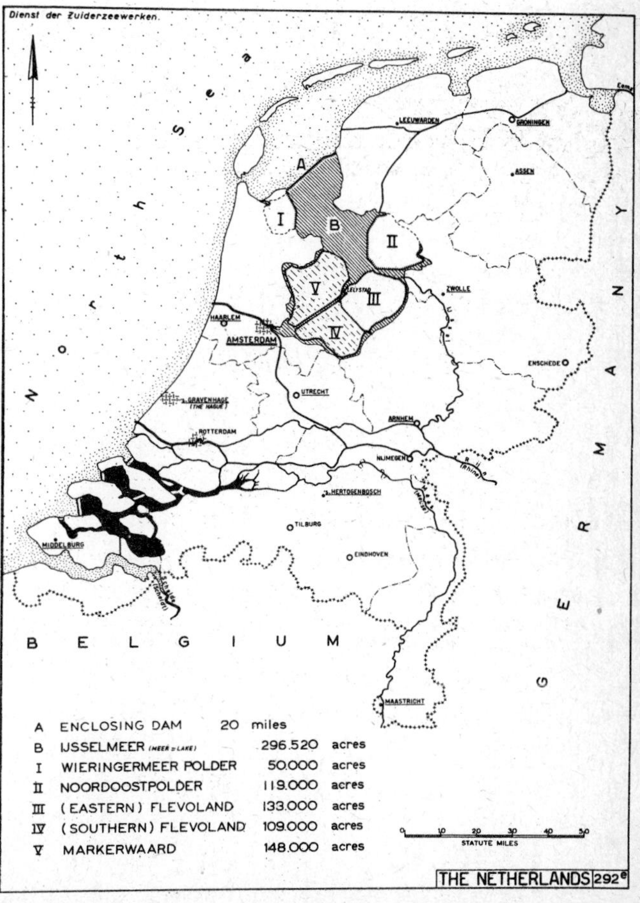

A far cry from the days of the windmills! This is one of the huge pumping stations on the Eastern Flevoland Polder.

Southern Flevoland and Markerwaard. As for the Zuyder Zee, it has ceased to exist, both in fact and in name. Now a fresh-water reservoir that ensures drinking water for much of Holland, it is known as the Ijsselmeer.

The reclamation programme hasn't always been as smooth as this article might suggest. In 1953, The Netherlands were struck by the worst floods in history, caused by excessive storms. The dykes were breached in several places, and $4\frac{1}{2}\%$ of the total area of the country went under water. Almost 1,800 people lost their lives, and over 70,000 more had to be evacuated. Altogether, one and half thousand million guilders' worth of damage was done, and in

An aerial view of the highway across the twenty-mile barrier-dam or 'Afsluitdijk' that keeps the North Sea out of Holland.

terms of pounds, that adds up to something like one hundred and seventy-five millions.

Men laboured day and night to close the gaps in the dykes—no doubt thinking bitterly of the old legend that tells of a young boy saving his country by putting his fist in a sea-wall breach! Some of the largest, most difficult gaps had to be closed with caissons . . . huge concrete supports weighing 7,000 tons each, and originally designed during the last war as disembarkation piers for the allied invasion of Europe.

Restoration took a whole year, and the Dutch Government began planning to make it impossible for such a disaster ever to happen again.

So began the Delta Project, in full swing today, which aims to control the scattered waters of the river estuaries in the south of Holland. The Dutch expect to complete this project in 1978, by which time there will be four huge dams across the deep sea inlets of Haringvliet, Brouwershavensche Gat, Ooster Scheldt and Veersche Gat.

The Cheese Market at Alkmaar, where Pete and Tony find that it's business as usual in a town that, like many in Holland, lies well below sea-level.

There'll be secondary dams across the Zandcreek, the Grevelingen and the Volkerak, and there'll be controlled inlets in the Rotterdam Waterway and the Western Scheldt to give shipping access to the major European ports of Rotterdam and Antwerp. There'll be a storm-barrier at Kapelle on the Ijssel, working like a huge sluice-gate to let out any dangerous build-up of water behind it that threatens the dykes.

There is a monument on the Afsluitdijk that turned the Zuyder Zee into Lake Ijssel. On it is inscribed a motto—"Een volk dat leeft, bouwt aan zinjn toekomst". It means 'A vigorous nation builds for its future'. There could be no better motto to describe the determination of the Dutch to conquer their old enemy, the sea. No, maybe not to conquer . . . just to pacify, and turn foe into friend. ■

Joyeux Noël

Fröhliche Weihnachten

GOD JU

MERRY CHRISTMAS

PRETTIGE KERSTDAGEN

С Новым Годом

Felices Fiestas

It doesn't matter what language you say it in, the seasonal wish is just the same. And what exactly do we think of when we talk about a merry Christmas? Holly and mistletoe? The giving of presents? Turkey and plum pudding and gaily coloured cards? Whatever it is, everything celebrates the birth of Jesus Christ, but even His birthday is shrouded in as much mystery as the origin of all our special customs!

Pete Brady

WHEN EXACTLY was Jesus born? It certainly wasn't on December 25th, and even if it had been, the manger wouldn't have been surrounded with dancing snowflakes and chirping robins. There wouldn't have been a holly bush in sight, and as for turkeys and plum puddings, the three kings, wise as they were supposed to have been, wouldn't even have heard of them.

No, the early Christians cashed in, as it were, on existing feasts to hold their own celebrations. Perhaps because everyone was in a holiday mood at the time, or perhaps because they could carry out their religious festivities without attracting the unwelcome attention of their enemies.

In the Western World, the end of December always signified a sort of climax . . . the time of year when the Sun, thin and cold after the hot summer, began its gradual return to warmth.

In pre-Christian times, people worshipped the Sun, and held great feasts in December to encourage it to come back to them and make their crops grow. They sincerely believed that revelry, held in the Sun's honour, pleased their fiery 'god'.

The traditions died hard, and when Christians began to spread the Gospel across Europe, they were sensible enough not to stamp out these pagan rites. Ordinary folk enjoyed their December celebrations, and they were encouraged to keep them—as long as they held them in honour of the Christian God rather than the Sun.

In much of Roman occupied Europe, the December festival was Saturnalia, seven days of merriment given to the appeasing of Saturn. People would be wildly extravagant, and spend money on fabulous parties. They would give each other gifts—often dolls called sigillaria. They would decorate their homes with evergreen boughs called strenae. These two customs continued through the spread of Christianity and persist even today.

Two of the long-established Christmas customs—the Yule Log and the mistletoe, are relics of much older religions brought to Britain by the Vikings, the Angles and the Saxons. The Vikings were brought up to revere fire—a fact that explains their notorious habit of burning the towns and villages they conquered. It seems that when there were no houses to ignite, they would make offerings to their nordic gods by burning boats, or failing that, great logs. These days, happily, most people who have open fires are content with the latter, although in Lerwick, in the Shetland Islands, a festival survives called Up Helly Aa, where, after Christmas, a longship is set afire. The words 'Up Helly Aa' mean, 'the end of the holiday', and locals in costume make the ceremony so realistic that their Dane-plagued forefathers probably spin in their graves!

As for mistletoe, it is a parasite that grows on parent trees, in ancient times used by the Druids as a cure for almost any disease. In Scandinavian mythology, it gave the wood that Lokai used to fashion the dart with which he slew Baldur. According to the early Christians, it was mistletoe

Christmas in Australia! Santa arrives through the surf at Bondi Beach . . . maybe his reindeer found the December sunshine too much for them!

The people of Lerwick in the Shetlands celebrate Up Helly Aa, an ancient Norse festival meaning the end of the holiday. They burn a Viking longboat in a tradition connected with burning the Yule Log.

wood that fashioned the cross—and because of the shame it felt, mistletoe ever afterwards became a shrivelled bunch of vegetation, doomed to depend on the solid oak tree for its life!

However, its tender green leaves and white berries became popular for the making of kissing boughs, beneath which perfect strangers could salute each other with a gesture of peace.

In the middle ages, no Christmas celebration was complete without the pudding. They called it plumb pudding—the word 'plumb' meaning heavy. It was nothing like our present-day pudding. In fact, it usually had chunks of meat in it, as well as dried prunes and hulled wheat. It wasn't round, and it didn't come flaming with brandy. It didn't even have a sprig of holly in it. But it went down just the same, along with a staggering menu of chickens, oxen, fish, and even roast peacocks for those who could afford such luxuries. The Christmas dinner in those days usually began in the morning and lasted well into the night—which must have meant chronic indigestion well into the new year!

In passing, we mustn't forget the mince pie, which was originally made of real mince, that is, shredded meat. In fact, it was called a 'shird pie', and its special feature was a crust specially made with a dip in the middle, to resemble a manger. There was always a little doll to represent the Christ Child, laid there.

It wasn't until Victorian times that the Christmas card came into being. Previously, people had been content to wish each other the compliments of the season as they met on their way to church, or passed each other in the street. But with the introduction of the penny post in 1840, friends and relatives separated by long distances began to write each other greetings letters. Some commercially-minded firms produced letter paper with Christmas wishes already printed at the head, but the card as such was invented by a man named John Calcott Horsley in 1843.

Horsley, an artist, drew the card at the express wish of Sir Henry Cole, a man who felt that he had insufficient strength in his wrist to write separate messages to all his acquaintances. The card proved a success, and went on the market at a shilling a copy. It seems that only a thousand or so were sold at first, but the idea caught on, and within a few years, firms were doing a thriving business with them.

Apart from the printed cards, there soon appeared ones lavishly decorated with silk and satin. Cards glittering with jewels, both mock and real; cards that squeaked when you pressed them; cards with holly and snow and stage coaches, and even cards in the comic vein—anticipating the main vogue today.

We've got one thing left concerning our modern Christmas—leaving aside the obvious religious aspect of the festival, that is. We've got crackers.

Never mind the jokes in them—they're just a little extra. As for the funny hats, they too date back to pagan times—especially to the 'feast of fools' we've mentioned earlier. They also symbolise, to a certain extent, the crowns of the three wise kings. But it's the noise crackers make that we're really interested in.

The 'snap' inside them that goes bang when you pull is related to the fire-crackers of ancient Chinese celebrations. The bang is a direct cousin to the tolling of church bells. It's a brother of the whistle you give when you're alone in the dark. Get the connection? It's *noise* . . . and noise was anciently supposed to drive away evil spirits! It's a jolly sound idea, really—if you'll pardon the pun. Pull the cracker and keep the party lively! Who wants evil spirits buzzing around that lovely turkey?

One last point. Do you believe in Santa Claus? Oh yes, he really existed. He was Saint Nicholas, a bishop of Myra in Asia Minor in the fourth century B.C. Apart from being the patron saint of sailors, thanks to his legendary control over storms, Saint Nicholas endeared himself to unmarried maidens. It's said that he saved three young girls from embarrassment. They were worried because their poor father hadn't enough money to provide their future husbands with dowries. Anyway, Saint Nicholas came along and threw a bag of gold into each of their bedroom windows, which made him popular enough to be remembered at the happiest time of the year—Christmas. So began the legend of his midnight sleigh-ride through the skies, bringing presents to every maiden—and, because they didn't want to be left out, every boy as well!

Anyway, whether you believe in Santa or not, and whether you hang about under the mistletoe or avoid it like the plague, we're all of us on MAGPIE going to wish you what we wish ourselves. A very, *very* merry Christmas indeed! ■

They're waiting for Santa . . . but who *was* Saint Nicholas?

The Christmas Tree came from Germany, where its evergreen leaves were a symbol of permanence.

They sting, they buzz, and they certainly are *busy. It's impossible to sit in a summer garden without noticing the little brown bodies flitting from flower to flower, poking about for nectar to take back to the comb. They're bees, of course, and unlike their yellow-and-black striped relatives the wasps, who are pretty useless scavengers, bees have more right to the title "man's best friend" than all the dogs in creation. The reason is very simple, for bees make honey, which is one of the best foods the human being can possibly have, being composed of pure, natural, energy-giving sugar.*

HONEY FOR TEA

BEES HAVE BEEN AROUND for an awful long time. Rock-paintings thousands of years old show them, and there are four distinct types scattered over the world. Here in Britain, we only see one kind—the Western honey-bee, but there are several different forms, all closely related. Some are large, some small. Some vary in colour; some have longer tongues. Again, some prefer working in colder weather than others . . . but they *all* produce honey, and most of them do the job in man-made hives.

Occasionally, you'll find a colony building a comb in the wild . . . a weird, mis-shapen yellowish bag hanging among thorny branches, looking like some dreadful monster from outer space . . . but bees actually prefer life in a hive, where they're protected from cold winter rain, which kills them.

In every hive, there are three types of bee. The worker (he's the chap you're likely to see buzzing round the garden) whose job in life is to build the honeycomb, to go out gathering nectar and pollen, to feed the Queen Bee, and to look after the eggs and larvae in the hive-cells; the Queen herself, who is rarely seen out of the hive, and whose job is simply to lay eggs; and lastly the drone . . . the true male bee, who is a lazy sort of beggar who crams down the food that the workers bring in, and hangs about waiting for his chance to mate with the Queen.

The Queen is naturally enough the central figure in any hive, and she is usually a direct descendant of a previous queen, raised from an egg laid in a special cell. Once she has assumed her throne, as it were, she leaves the hive and goes on her wedding flight . . . the only occasion when you are likely to see her. She's quite distinct from other bees thanks to her long, tapered

A worker bee using its head as a hammer to pack pollen into a storage cell. Pollen is used as food for the young.

body, and you needn't be afraid of a sting from her, for she keeps it to use solely against any rival queens who dare to threaten her authority!

She flies high and strongly, and drone bees chase her like eager suitors, running a sort of race to catch her. Later, she returns to the hive, and settles down to the rest of her life's work, which is laying eggs. Perhaps she's the busiest of the busy bees, for she has to lay 2,000 or more eggs every day!

In the meantime, the worker bees have constructed the cells in extremely scientific fashion. Such and such a shape for producing more workers, a different dimension for drones and yet another for future queens. The eggs hatch after three days, and the workers are rushed off their six feet to keep a supply of food coming in. They feed the larva directly from glands in their heads, but they always have a surplus to store in the hive for later use. So begins the gradual build-up of honey . . . enough for all the bees to last over the winter, and enough for the bee-keeper to take away besides!

The comb itself is made of beeswax, which the workers produce from glands on their stomachs. Small flakes come off, which are chewed and built into the beautifully geometric patterns you can see in any honeycomb. It takes over ten pounds of sugar to make one pound of beeswax, so you can understand why bee-keepers save all the spare wax they can find to process into foundations for his hive frames. He wants the bees to spend as much time making honey as they can, and never mind about the wax!

The workers have a very regimented system of producing honey. From the flowers they take nectar, a sweet, sugary liquid that the flowers produce simply to attract insects to them. They suck up the liquid and take it back to the hive, where it is passed to other bees who convert it into simpler, thicker sugars for storage. As for the pollen which the bees gather, some of it rubs from their legs to fertilise other flowers (clever flowers—they produced nectar in the first place so that the bees would come and do the fertilisation job for them) but much of it goes back to the hive as well, for packing into special cells as direct food for young larvae.

It's around the end of July, when there is not much opportunity for the bees to gather more nectar, that the bee-keeper will consider taking the surplus honey from the hive. He has to be sure to leave enough for the bees' winter needs, or else they will starve in the spring . . . but every good keeper knows exactly how much to take. He puts a special apparatus into the hive which allows the bees to pass out of the honeycombs, but not to return to them, and after a couple of days, he takes out the combs he wants and replaces the racks with new ones. He keeps himself from being stung by hanging a special netted hat over his head, and he usually carries a smoke-producer that keeps the bees drowsy.

You might think that bees are a bit soft to spend their lives working so hard when half their effort goes to feeding mankind . . . but in actual fact they're among the most intelligent of insects. The discipline of the hive is as tight as that in an army unit, and the bees even have a means of communicating with each other . . . in the language of the dance!

When worker bees, on their own, discover a particularly good source of nectar, they come back to the hive and 'entertain' the others on the surface of the comb. If the food is less than a hundred yards from the hive they do 'the round dance'—jigging about in a perfect circle, backwards and forwards. If it's farther away than that, they do 'the waggle dance'—consisting of curious semi-circles, with much body-waggling thrown in! Even more remarkable, the directions in which the bees do these dances tell their comrades exactly in which direction to fly to reach the prize!

Incidentally, if reading all this makes you so fascinated by bees that you simply have to drop your bread and honey to pop out and have a closer look, be careful of getting stung. It's not likely to hurt you much, and a sliced onion or some lemon juice will probably ease the discomfort . . . but the poor bee—which only did it in self defence, after all—is likely to die afterwards. A dreadfully undeserved fate for one of man's best friends! □

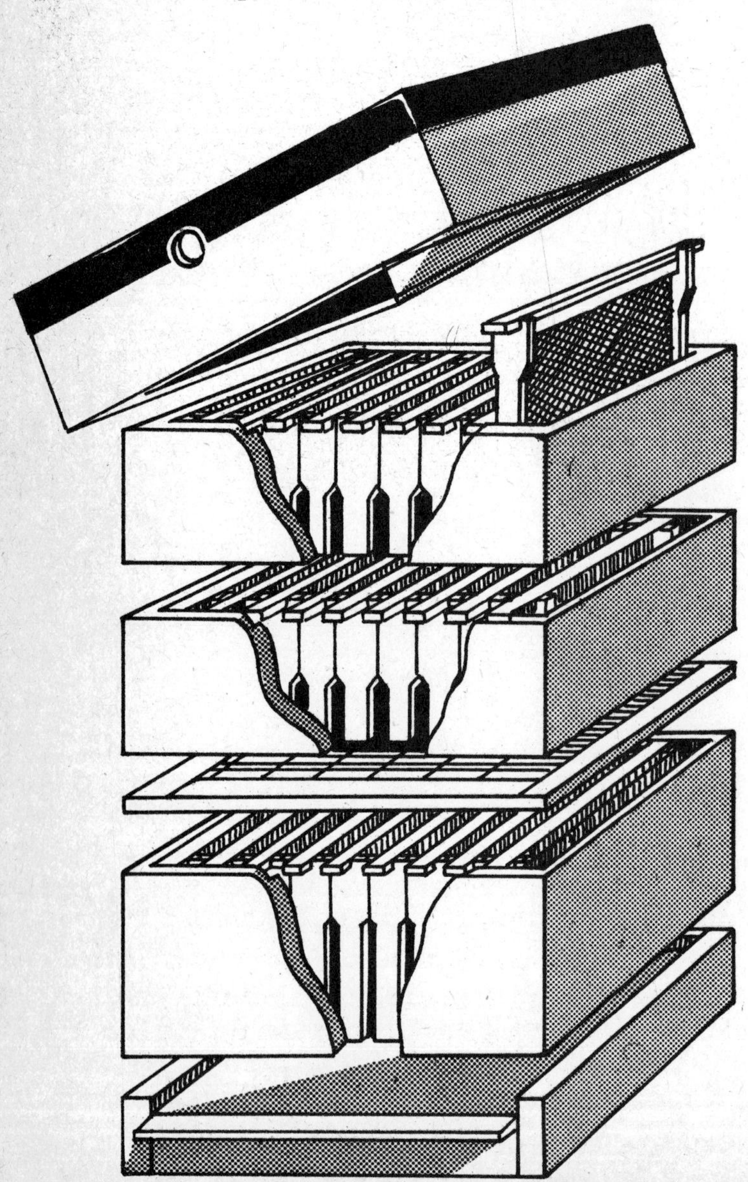

A TYPICAL BEE-HIVE, SECTION BY SECTION

The top section is the roof, and is covered with felt or zinc. It has mesh ventilator holes on each side. The next two sections are honey boxes, each containing frames of wax honeycomb to give the bees a start. Then comes a slotted or wired Queen excluder, which permits worker bees to pass through, but not the Queen.
Then there's the brood box, with tall frames of wax honeycomb, and finally the floor section, into which is built the opening through which bees can leave and return to the hive.

COME TO THE CIRCUS

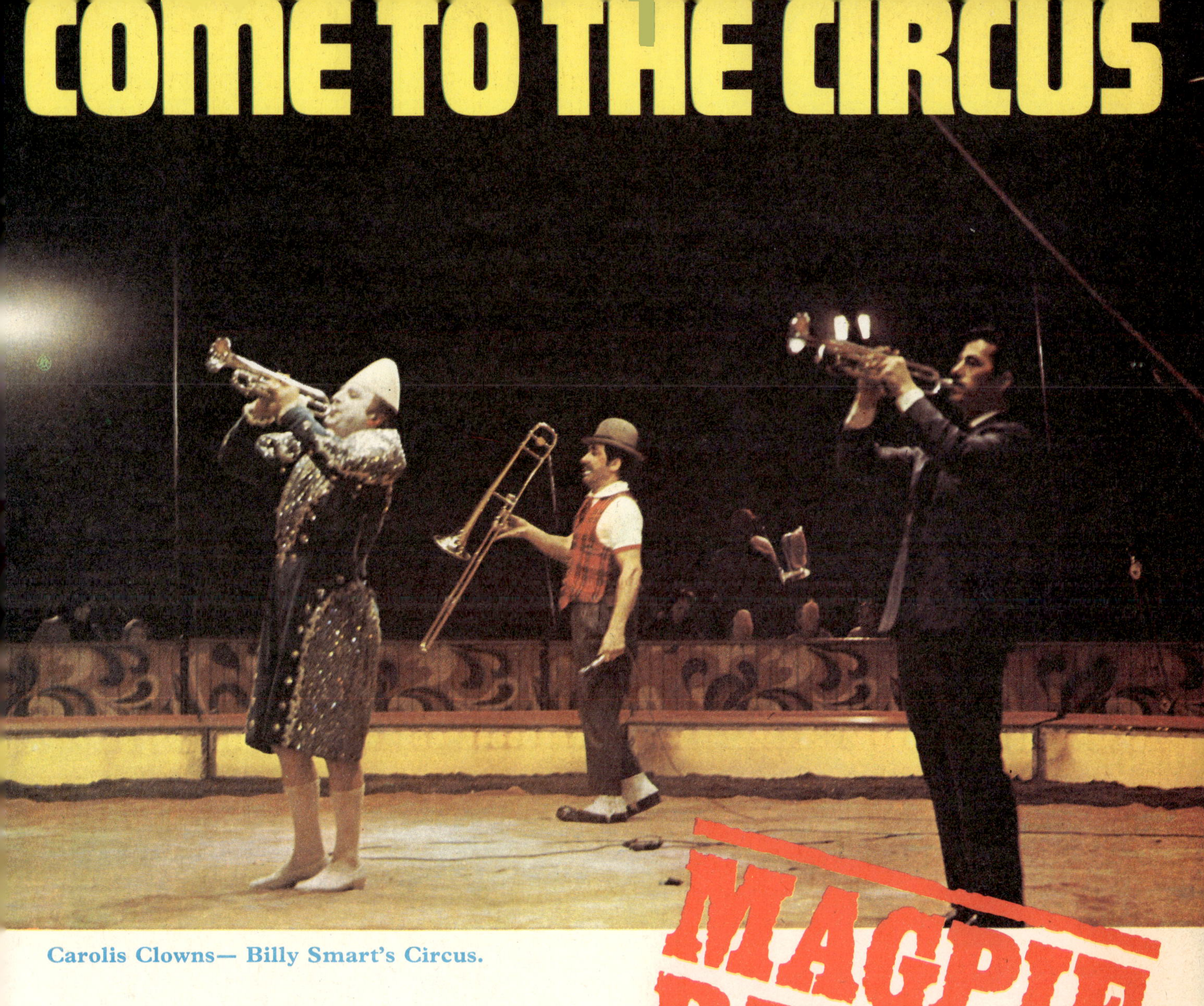

Carolis Clowns— Billy Smart's Circus.

MAGPIE REPORT

There they were, a Ponger and a Slanger. Both as different as chalk and cheese, but both real Bona Omeys. Confused? So was I, before I knew about the private language of the circus—a baffling mish-mash of terms borrowed from Italian, French, Romany and goodness knows what else! The Ponger, to me, was an acrobat. As for the Slanger, he turned out to be an animal trainer! The other bit? Well, a Bona Omey is simply a good man!

Apart from the language, there's a wealth of tradition in the circus, and I'd like to tell you something about it. Naturally, I don't personally belong to the circus . . . which makes me a Flattie! Nevertheless, Flattie or not, here goes. . . .

Tony Bastable

THE WORD "CIRCUS" is Latin, and it merely describes the round form of the early Roman amphitheatres, where games were frequently held for the pleasure of Caesar and commoner alike. The games weren't exactly circuses as we know them today, although there were a number of

acts devoted to trick horseback riding. The normal show included such delicate exhibitions as battles to the death between captive enemy soldiers and wild beasts, and the whole thing was generally accepted to be an excuse for satisfying the bloodthirsty nature of the crowd!

The Romans brought the word "circus" to England with them, but over the years it lost its special meaning. There were plenty of performers around of the sort we see today . . . jugglers, acrobats, contortionists and equestrians. But they were all independent wanderers, travelling from town to town and fair to fair.

There were "glee-men", too—poor buffoons who had to caper and gibber to earn a copper or two for food.

It wasn't until 1768 that, in an area between Blackfriars and Westminster known as Halfpenny Hatch, a character by the name of Philip Astley gave the first ever "circus-as-we-know-it" performance in the world. In fact, he didn't call it a circus. He called it a "riding school". But a circus it was, for all that, and soon Astley—an ex-

Left: The Reynoso Trio performing another daring feat.

Below: An old print depicting Astley's Royal Grove and Amphitheatre, Riding House, Westminster Bridge.

John Gindl with Billy Smart's Circus Horses.

sergeant-major with atrocious manners and little education—proved that he had a real talent for showmanship, by drawing enormous crowds to witness trick riding, the antics of clowns and performing dogs, the skill of jugglers and rope-walkers and the contortions of tumblers. Astley and his wife were themselves spectacular horseback performers, and the great man's star turn was to balance upside down on a pint-pot resting on his horse's saddle . . . at full gallop! It's said the trick vastly impressed King George III, and Philip Astley certainly found himself to be a unique centre of attraction!

Not for long! Anyone who makes a success of something new is bound to end up with rivals, and Astley was no exception. To his rage, a man named Charles Hughes set up in opposition, and open warfare instantly broke out between the two circuses. Hughes raised Astley's blood-pressure by advertising an act in which the rider balanced upside down, at the gallop, on "a whole *galaxy* of pint-pots". Astley countered by roofing over his whole circus. Hughes replied by building his magnificent Royal Circus in Blackfriars Road. And so on, and so on.

Hughes fell into debt, and died. His circus burned down, and once more Philip Astley was without a rival. He took his show to Europe, where it caused a sensation. He added more and more acts, put on bigger and better extravaganzas, and died at the height of his fame, leaving the circus to his son John, who lived long enough to see the circus become established as popular entertainment. By now, many of the acts who had begun their work at Astley's had broken away to form circuses on their own. Paris had its own Circus Olympique; American audiences were thrilling to the spectacles of the ring; men like John Clarke, Abraham Saunders, Andrew Ducrow and George E. Stephenson were

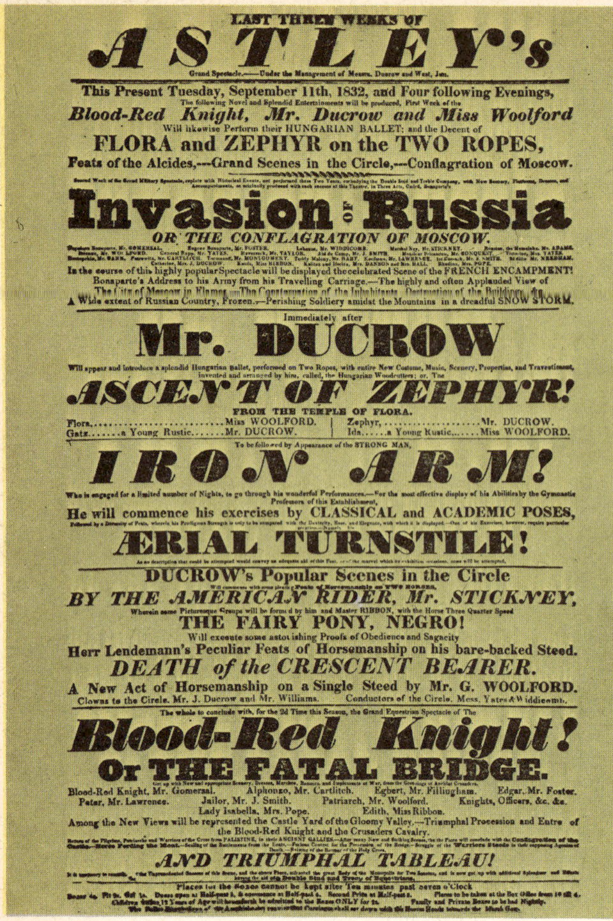

An early poster advertising Astley's "Circus".

busily building the traditions of big-time circus showmanship that survive today in magic names Chipperfield, Mills and Smart.

By far one of the best remembered names in old-time British circus is that of Sanger. "Lord" George Sanger.

The son of a minor showman who had once served on Nelson's flagship Victory at Trafalgar, George Sanger began work early. At five years old he was "barking"—calling in customers—for the family sideshow in a travelling fair. By the time he was in his twenties, he was on his own, and his quick eye for anything new set him on the road to fame. He found a journeyman metalworker in Huddersfield who had invented a naphtha lamp that burned with a much brighter flame than ordinary oil lamps. Accordingly, he illuminated his circus with naphtha, and people who came to see the amazing invention stayed for the show, and went away doubly impressed!

Sanger lived up to that oldest of circus rules . . . "The show must go on". On one occasion in Norwich, the chemist's assistant who supplied gases for the circus illuminations made a mistake, and a resultant explosion blew the Sangers' living quarters to bits, dangerously burning both the showman and his wife. Doctors were rushed to help them, but while the first aid was going on, thieves sneaked in and ran off with the circus takings! The citizens of Norwich were immensely sympathetic. They offered to raise funds for Sanger. But like the man of character he was, he refused charity, and insisted that he continued working!

Lord George Sanger ("Lord" was a nickname he'd earned for his elegant manners and gentlemanly behaviour) took his circus all over Britain and the continent. As a travelling tent show it grew enormous, and the long parade of gaily painted wagons was a breath-taking sight in itself for any villagers or townsfolk lucky enough to live along the route. As a sort of home base, Sanger bought Astley's old amphitheatre in London, and proceeded to put on shows that would have drawn gasps of admiration from Astley himself. In one 'spectacular', seven-hundred men, women and children appeared in the ring at once . . . *plus* thirteen elephants, nine camels, fifty-two horses and two lions. Oh yes, and just to make it all really crowded, a miscellany of ostriches, kangaroos, reindeer, pelicans and so on and so on!

Like that of Sanger, the name of Bertram Mills has become inseparably attached to the word "circus". The son of a coach-builder, Mills entered the circus business by pure chance. He'd always been fascinated by horses, and in 1919, he went with a friend to see a circus at Olympia. Afterwards, his friend asked Mills what he'd thought of the show, and Mills replied: "If I couldn't put on a better circus that that, I'd eat my hat." Back came the challenge: "Back up those words, Bertram. I'll bet you a hundred pounds you can't." Anyway, Bertram Mills *did!*

It wasn't easy. At first, he tried to bring the famous Ringling, Barnum and Bailey circus across from America, but that arrangement fell through thanks to transport difficulties. So Bertram Mills set off on a continental tour, talent-spotting, booking up acts to bring back. The success of his circus was immediate, and Mills was soon master of a gay, gaudy travelling road show that had all of the Sanger glitter about it. Who could resist the parade of bandsmen through a town? The prancing liberty horses, the swaying elephants, the tumbling, capering clowns? Everything about such a procession was literally out of this world. There was nothing there that could be encountered in day-to-day life . . . and therein lay its whole *magic!*

But is it all magic to the people of the circus themselves? We're always hearing about the sad clown whose happy face is only painted on. What about these circus entertainers and the life they lead? *Is* it all just a humdrum job to them?

Not a bit of it! Just look in, if ever you get the chance, at a circus making ready to move out of winter quarters! There's laughter and talking and whistling, and the industrious noise of hammer and saw. There's a smell of paint in the air, and washing-lines are fluttering with a brilliant dazzle of airing costumes. Harness and trappings are being polished and renovated, and here and there animal trainers put their dogs, their horses, their chimps through one final rehearsal. There's no gloom here . . . everyone seems to be infected with that marvellous sense of 'up and doing' that comes with the springtime!

And on the road . . . even when the rain's bucketing down and the pitch (the "tober", they call it) is axle deep in brown mud . . . even when there's half a dozen gales blowing and the Big Top's driving everyone crazy . . . the laughter never stops. Two shows a day, nine months in the year. And only Sundays off. It takes a very special temperament to stand that sort of life, which is why circus people *are* so very special. They're showmen, all of them. They wouldn't be in the profession if they weren't.

Lord George Sanger.

They're tough. Take the trapeze artiste, Fritzi Bartoni. She fell thirty feet to the stage during practice, but went on to do the show . . . and it wasn't until later that a doctor discovered she'd fractured her pelvis!

Take Schumann, whose horse kicked his knee out of joint. He just ordered one of the hands to sit on his ankle while he yanked the bones back into place . . . and got up to finish the act.

Or, sad though it is, the most dramatic example of a circus performer's dedication to the ring. The story of Jean Clermont the clown, who went out to make the crowd delirious with laughter at his antics . . . just minutes after his little daughter had died in his arms.

There's tradition for you. A tradition that's as alive and kicking today, just as hard as it did at Astley's in 1768. They're bona omies all right, these folk of the circus.

ORIGAMAGPIE!

NO, IT'S NOT A MAGIC WORD like Abracadabra! It's just a bit of made-up nonsense to describe this gay-looking magpie, that you can easily make for yourself simply by folding a square of paper!

The art of paper-folding has long had a pretty world-wide following, its devotees frequently being professional conjurers interested in getting special effects into their acts. In Japan, it enjoyed a national sort of popularity, and under its Japanese name 'Origami', it became a hobby craze a few years ago.

For your model magpie, you need a square of white paper, the ideal size being about eight inches by eight. Remember, it *must* be perfectly square!

First, you fold the paper in half, diagonally, as in figure 1. Now fold points 'A' and 'B' up to point 'C' as shown in figure 2.

Tuck edges 'D' and 'E' inside the flaps until their tips meet on the centre line, and your paper should appear as it does in figure 3. The next step is to fold the whole thing in half down the centre line.

Figure 4 makes clear what the model looks like at this stage, and also shows a dotted line to indicate the next fold.

Take point 'B' and fold on that dotted line, so that you end up with the shape as in figure 5. Then turn the model over and do the same with point 'A', so that 'A' and 'B' are together as in figure 6. At this point, you may find it easier to tilt the model on its tum, and ink in some details . . . a nostril, an eye and a foot on each side. Now you can see more or less what the finished product is going to look like!

Finally, all you have to do is experiment with your own folds, pushing the head (point 'F') down to make it flat, bending the tail flat at 'C', turning the wings down a little. A paperclip, a small pin, or even a little loop of cotton pushed in just behind the wings will keep the whole thing rigid, and you can finish off by painting the magpie a dazzling black and white in any pattern you choose, with some yellow paint for the beak and feet. If you care to make three or four, you can hang them from your lampshade with some cotton, and watch them fly about in the draught!

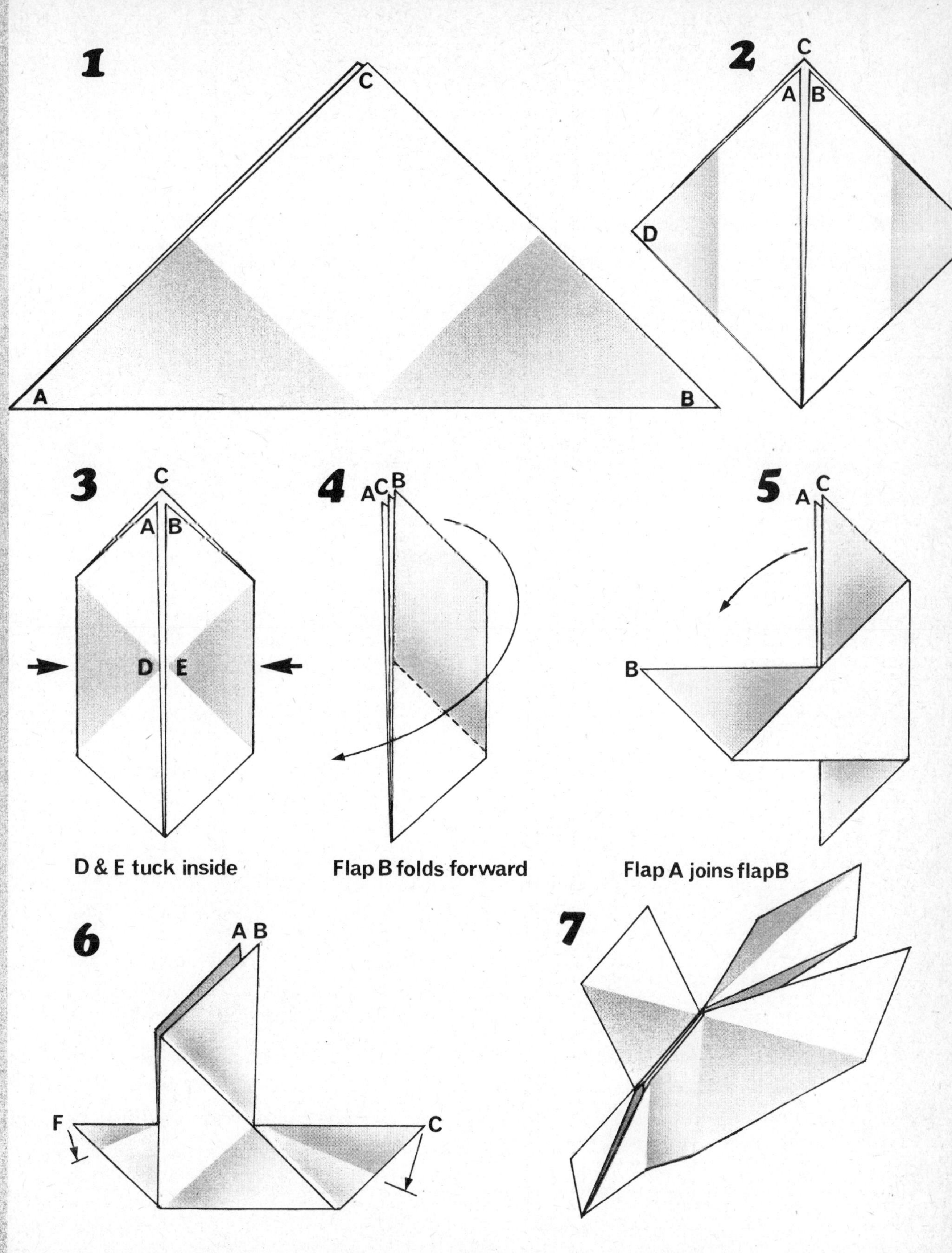
1
C
A
B
2
C
A
B
D
E
3
C
A
B
D
E
D & E tuck inside
4
A
C
B
Flap B folds forward
5
A
C
B
Flap A joins flapB
6
A
B
F
C
7

MY FOUR-FOOT

A CHAP LIKE ME is bound to have lots and lots of friends, really. I know I'm only twelve and a bit hands high, and I know I can be naughty sometimes, especially when I see something that's orange in colour! Orange things look tasty to me, you see . . . so you can't blame me for having a nibble.

My best friends are Susan, Tony and Pete, because they're so nice to me. In fact, everyone that's got anything to do with the Magpie programme—and that includes you, of course—have done wonders helping to forget the unhappier days when I was just a little pony, having to work hard for my living down in Wales. Perhaps they called me Puff when they rescued me, because I was always puffed out from being made to pull heavy wagons around!

Anyway, now I'm a television pony, and since Susan, Tony and Pete are having their say in this annual, I jolly well want mine, too! I'm not conceited, so I'm not going to blow my own trumpet. Instead, I'm going to tell you about some of the horsey friends I've made on my travels for Magpie. In fact, I'm going to tell you about some working horses who enjoy what they do and get the sort of loving treatment that any animal deserves, into the bargain!

I remember the time they took me down to the South Western suburbs of London, to a place called Wandsworth. It's a busy, noisy sort of place, but I wasn't frightened, although as you know I come from the Welsh hills, where the only sounds some of my brothers and sisters hear is the soft whisper of the wind and the chattering of stony streams. But noise doesn't frighten me, because I understand about what is making it. After all, I get plenty of practice in the 'Magpie' studio. I could smell the wide-open spaces of Wimbledon Common, not far away, and by the time I was trotted into the friendly, homely stables behind Young's Brewery, I felt absolutely at home!

You see, Young's are almost as famous for their twenty-two handsome Shire geldings as they are for their beers. They win prizes with both!

The Shires are awfully noble, and they look enormous to me! They're about seventeen hands on average—that's seventeen times four inches at the shoulder, to you. What? Your arithmetic's as bad as mine? All right, then—they're five feet, eight inches at the shoulder, while I'm only four feet two. (Tony did the sum for me!)

The Young's Shires do three journeys a day, pulling 'drays' loaded with barrels of beer. They deliver to the brewery's public houses within a three-mile radius of Wandsworth, and they look so marvellous in their gleaming brass and leather harness that even impatient motorists who get held up behind them don't seem to mind.

There's a team of Show-Shires, too, and Young's put them on display at the Royal Windsor, The Royal Richmond, The International Horse Show, and lots more . . . even shows as far away as Blackpool. They win masses of first prizes and championships, and so they should, because they're as smart as paint in their black coats and white socks. One of them told me he weighs over a ton, so I hope he'll never lean on the judges if they don't like him!

Shires were called The Great Horse of England back in the Middle Ages, when they were used as mounts for knights in heavy armour. They had to carry anything up to twenty stone into battle, and even if they were used for peaceful jobs, they had to be able to pull rough, heavy carts without springs over rutted tracks.

Some of the Young's geldings are show-

D FRIENDS!

Always admired, at work or in the show ring! These are my friends the Young's Brewery Shires.

business horses like me. A few of them are terribly proud of having been photographed with models for leading fashion magazines, and others have actually been film stars!

When I left Wandsworth, I just caught sight of some other handsome horses leaving the stables behind the local police station, but they were far too busy for me to talk to, and I had to wait until I was taken down to the place where all the Metropolitan Police horses are trained. Imber Court, in Surrey.

Police horses are friendly, and patient, and absolutely fearless. They have to be, because of the job they do. But of course they don't start out that way! Now, *I'm* not especially nervous. I can put up with the noise of a television studio, and all the bright lights, and all the people hurrying about here and there waving sheaves of paper. But when I had a go at one of the police-horse training routines, and allowed myself to be led between lines of policemen in outlandish clothes, waving flags, rattling rattles, and pushing around great oil-drums full of clattery stones, I wasn't at all sure of myself! They told me afterwards that I was much calmer than they expected, but I was really being brave and well-behaved because I didn't want the other horses to laugh at me.

The Metropolitan Police Mounted Branch has about two hundred horses on duty today, and most of them are bred in Yorkshire. They all come to Imber Court untrained, and they stay there until they have become quiet and placid, able to respond to the instructions of their riders under all sorts of irritating conditions. They have to be taught not to be nervous in traffic, and they have to learn to remain absolutely steady even in the middle of one of those horrible demonstrations, where placards are waved in their faces and fireworks are even thrown around.

Their training course is split into three parts, and the first is just a matter of hand-

All part of the training! *BANG!* And they won't move a muscle!

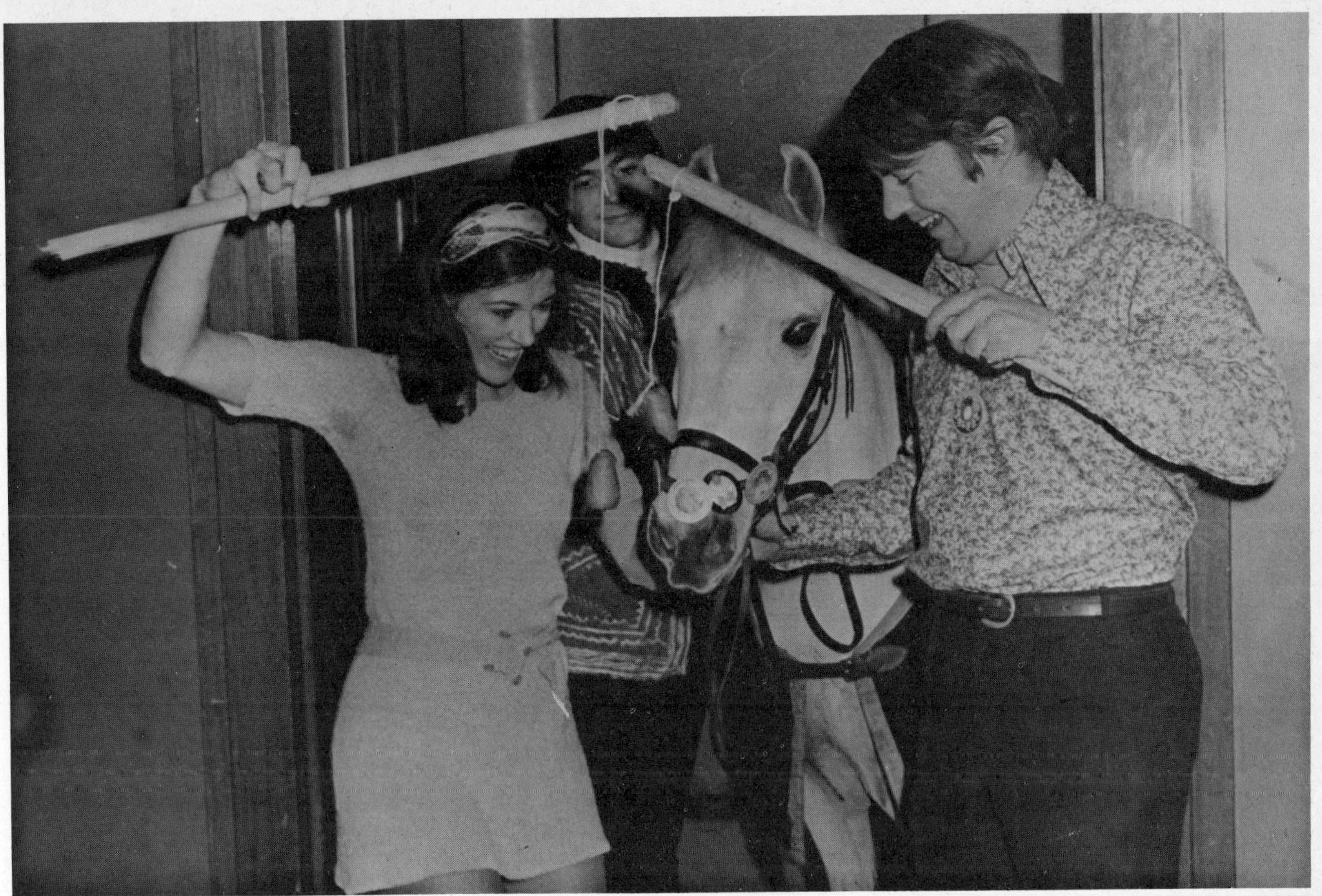

It takes a *really* smart pony to demand *two* carrots before he'll come out of a lift!

ling and driving. One of them told me that the object was to develop his character and his muscles, so that he'd be able to cope with more difficult second and third stages.

The second stage begins with the horse being mounted for the first time, and as soon as he's used to his rider, he's introduced to crowds, flags and rattles so that he can grow accustomed to the sort of thing he'll experience on ceremonial occasions. The third stage involves blaring bands, and what they call 'advanced training with crowds'—bells, bangs and so on.

The training is all very kind, and the idea is to accustom the horses to noise in gradual stages, so that they're never alarmed or frightened. For example, with music, the horses are just trotted round while radiograms and loudspeakers relay the noise to them . . . quietly at first, and then a bit louder, day by day. When they come to flags and rattles, they're placed in a large circle, where they can all see the men who are kicking up a shindy. It's all very gentle at first, and the horses are rewarded with oats to keep them happy!

Eventually, the flags and rattles are brought nearer to them, until they learn completely to ignore them. They come to accept all the fooling about in the end, even when the rewards of oats are done away with. That'd be the difficult thing for me, because I *like* oats, even when they don't come in orange feed-tins!

Like the police horses, I had a go at walking down between lines of men blowing trumpets, firing pistols, banging drums and generally capering about. I did my best to copy the advanced trainees by staying calm while they walked me through gates and over disconcerting surfaces like piled rubber cushions and bits of wood. But it was all jolly difficult. If I wore a hat, I'd take it off to those smart, polished-looking horses who take it all in their daily stride! ■

– IN MEDIÆVAL MANOR

"VERILY, let the feast begin!" It seems as though Pete Brady, Susan Stranks and Tony Bastable have stepped back to Elizabethan times to enjoy all the revelry of a banquet in a mediaeval manor house. But could these really be their illustrious ancestors Master Peter (newly arrived from the New World), Milady Susan (a notable lady often to be seen at the Queen's court) and Master Tony, the notable wit whose pen is said to rival that of Master Will Shakespeare? Let's just say that Studio 3 at Teddington lays on a marvellous imitation of a Tudor manor!

THERE were plenty of wenches in attendance to serve the food and the drink (it seems rude today, but in those days it was quite in order to bellow "wench!" when you needed serving). A banquet like this was many courses long—each course being a full meal by modern standards.

WITH a banquet taking many hours, tempers were bound to become frayed! Here, John Waller of the Mediaeval Society—sorry, *Master* John Waller—claims his soup is cold. Master Peter Brady takes the unfortunate wench's side, but Master John Asmus (also of the Mediaeval Society) stands up to make a real issue of things! You can see the swords and daggers on the table already!

IT WAS quite commonplace for even the slightest meal-table arguments to come to a stand-up sword-fight. Usually, the guests not involved would try their level best to calm the opponents down!

AH! They've made it up again (even if the swords *are* still on the board, ready for the next time!). You'll see there wasn't much conventional cutlery around . . . normally a knife and spoon for each guest, and very occasionally a fork as well. But often food was eaten with the fingers, and a pitcher of water stood ready for anyone whose hands became too greasy. Nobody ever drank water . . . they'd probably have died of pestilence if they had! The table drinks were mead (made from fermented honey), beer or wine—generally consumed in gallons!

ENTER Puff, in the company of Milady Pauline Voss (mistress of the Magpie Pony). He'd have been quite welcome in the straw-scattered banqueting hall, since animals were normally allowed into any household.

THE banquet over, guests and servants alike gather round the lute-playing minstrel who has been supplying continuous entertainment throughout the feast. In view of the time of year (actually it was the end of 1969, and you may have seen the transmission), everyone joins in a Christmas song of well-wishing. To be honest, it was an Elizabethan version of "We wish you a merry Christmas and a Happy New Year".

How did you make out...?

Murgatroyd's Mind-Bogglers

① Answers to Mind-Bogglers on page 21

'A'—A zip fastener.
'B'—A light-bulb filament.
'C'—A tin-opener.
'D'—A half of grapefruit.

② Answers to Mind-Bogglers on page 34

(a) The pictures.

'A'—An apple stalk.
'B'—The top of a pepper-pot.
'C'—A pile of coins on edge.
'D'—Coat Button.
'E'—Bread.

(b) Imagine the results of an English grammar test at school. This sentence describes the result:
"Bill, while Tom had had 'had', had had 'had had'. 'Had had' had had the teacher's approval."

(c) The man is a father looking at a portrait of his own son.

WIN YOUR OWN SPOT

ON TELEVISION !

JUST IMAGINE! You're a V.I.P. for the day! Taken down to the Thames Television studios at Teddington Lock, introduced to all the people who work to put MAGPIE on the screen! You'll meet the presenters face to face, chat with Sue Turner, the programme's producer, *and* appear yourself on the live transmission of the afternoon show! Just think what your friends will say when they see *your* face on their TV screens!

How does this dream come true? Just enter our simple competition, and keep your fingers crossed that you win!

HERE'S WHAT YOU HAVE TO DO:

See the photograph of Susan, Tony and Pete, with the tame magpie perched on Sue's shoulder? Well, try and think of something witty that the magpie might be saying to them—speaking as a *real* magpie in terms of our programme's own Murgatroyd!

Just make up your own humorous comment, and fill it into the empty balloon on the picture.

When you're satisfied that it's as funny as you can make it, copy the remark down on a postcard, like this:

The magpie is saying: " . . . . " (write your suggestion here).

Be sure to print your full name and address on the postcard, and send it to

MAGPIE ANNUAL COMPETITION,
THAMES TELEVISION LTD,
TELEVISION HOUSE,
KINGSWAY, LONDON W.C.2.

RULES OF THE COMPETITION

Entries must arrive before 1 March 1971 otherwise they will automatically be disqualified.

Entries meeting the requirements of the competition will be put together and judged by the presenters. The entry they judge to be the cleverest and funniest will be declared the winner.

The judges' decision will be final and no correspondence can be entered into concerning this competition. The winner will be notified by post before 1 April 1971.

The right to publish the winning entry is reserved and it is regretted that no entries can be returned to the authors or otherwise.

Entry is excluded to employees and families of the Publisher, Associated Companies, Thames Television Ltd and the printers.

One for Sorrow
Two for Joy
Three for a Girl
And Four for a Boy
Five for Silver
Six for Gold
Seven for a Secret
never to be told